TEXAS CAESAR

DARRELL K ROYAL | 1924-2012

J. BRENT CLARK

abbott press

Abbott Press books may be ordered through booksellers or by contacting:

Abbott Press
1663 Liberty Drive
Bloomington, IN 47403
www.abbottpress.com
Phone: 1 (866) 697-5310

ISBN: 978-1-4582-1940-4 (sc)
ISBN: 978-1-4582-1942-8 (hc)
ISBN: 978-1-4582-1941-1 (e)

Print information available on the last page.

Abbott Press rev. date: 09/25/2015

OTHER BOOKS BY J. BRENT CLARK

3rd Down & Forever: Joe Don Looney and the Rise and Fall of an American Hero

Sooner Century: 100 Glorious Years of Oklahoma Football

Royal Family Collection

TABLE OF CONTENTS

PREFACE

My son had earned the right to make his own decision. After all, he'd excelled at Oklahoma City's Casady School, finishing as a National Merit Scholar. Now it was time for him to choose a university. I'd loved the University of Oklahoma all my life to the extent that my two sons and I had continued to live walking distance from the OU campus. I confided to a close friend that even though I'm in my sixties, I still get a lump in my throat when the Pride of Oklahoma marching band takes the field at football games and marches to the state song, "Oklahoma." I assumed, mistakenly, that my son would arrive at the conclusion that OU was the best place for him. Out of the blue, without having visited the UT campus, he announced he wanted to attend the University of Texas in Austin. He explained, "It's a big school......a diverse place....fine academics...it'll be an adventure....I'll be on my own."

Moving-in day was the first of many adventures we would have as a family. The private dormitory near the "Drag," Guadalupe Avenue, was co-ed. His male roommates were the product of on-line matching-nothing more. A quartet of girls had already moved in next door although I never met them. I could hear their giggling through the wall and sensed the smell of pot coming from underneath their door. After I shared the obligatory pizza lunch with my son, I hugged him and headed back to Norman.

On the six-hour drive, I thought a lot about what lay ahead for our family. I thought back to my youth, growing up in Holdenville, Oklahoma, a small county seat town. Before I was old enough to travel with my parents to Dallas for OU-Texas weekend, I helped decorate my parents' Pontiac in red and white crepe paper for their drive on Friday afternoon. Their friends were doing the same with their cars as well. The idea of a caravan of Sooner fans to Dallas was an annual event to be eagerly anticipated. Besides, Oklahoma was a dry state while Texas was wet. My dad would buy bourbon by the case in Dallas to be hidden in the trunk before heading home. It was much better than dealing with the bootlegger at the cab stand in nearby Wewoka. As long as I can remember, we all wanted OU to "beat the hell outa Texas." Before regular television broadcasts of the game, I'd sit close to the radio, more often than not, fidgeting with the football I'd won in a raffle at Woods Grocery Store. One phrase that sticks in my mind after over fifty years is the radio play-by-play announcer repeatedly saying, "Lackey under," referring to the fine Texas quarterback, Bobby Lackey. In my youth, Texas seemed so huge—so prosperous---and yes, so superior in every way. Defeating the Texas Longhorns in the intense annual rivalry game somehow validated us as equals. It wasn't any more complicated than that. We didn't talk about it. It was just something we felt intensely. My growing up didn't alter this fundamental objective of proving myself vicariously through the play of the Oklahoma Sooners every October. The Sooners were going to defend honor for themselves, the University, the State and me.

My son had been attending all OU home games since he was old enough to sit through a game. He also had been to every OU-Texas weekend over the same period. He'd been thoroughly indoctrinated by all those around him. For years our road trip down I-35 to Dallas included a stopover at the "Bevo Bash," an ad hoc gathering of Sooner fans in the Arbuckle Mountains. We'd get interviewed on the mobile Sooner radio broadcast and by instinct, predict a Sooner rout of the Horns. The Bash attracted enough attention that capitalism eventually took over, moving it to a fast food restaurant in Pauls Valley, thus killing its marvelous impromptu energy. I wondered what was in store for my son in the days and years ahead. How was he going to be able to reconcile conflicting feelings for OU and UT? How would he be accepted by his classmates in Austin once he announced he was from Norman, Oklahoma? What was in store for us when we'd meet in Dallas each October for the weekend? I knew I had to prepare to see him decked out in burnt orange. It was going to be alright, I told myself.

My son surprised me. In retrospect, he demonstrated character beyond what I had thought possible. Over his four years of undergrad school in Austin, he flourished. His academic achievements were superior. His social life was wonderful, including membership in Absolute Texxas, a co-ed social organization of several hundred members. (The organization was famous for its pre-game tailgates.) My son was so enthusiastic about UT that for three years running, he served as a counselor for Camp Texas, a weeklong orientation retreat for incoming UT freshmen. The kid from Oklahoma was doing just fine. After four years, he graduated from UT with highest honors in neurobiology and was off to medical school. And every October, he met his family in Dallas, wearing his favorite crimson and cream Oklahoma Sooners shirt. I was so proud of him, not because he cheered for OU, but because of the man he had become.

When Darrell K Royal passed away November 7, 2012, his funeral attracted thousands to the Erwin Center on the UT campus. I read all of the obituaries, which talked about his accomplishments as a college football player and as a Hall of Fame college football coach. I read that he would be laid to rest in Texas State Cemetery in Austin, near governors and senators and titans of Texas industry and commerce. I was aware that like me, Darrell had grown up in a small county seat town, Hollis, Oklahoma. He had listened to

OU football games on the radio in the days before television, all the while dreaming of playing for the Sooners, just like I had. Today, the mammoth football stadium on the UT campus is named "Darrell K Royal Texas Memorial Stadium."

How could this be? I choose to believe that Darrell K Royal was a person of uncommon character, flawed perhaps, by blind ambition. He was a dreamer. He loved his Oklahoma roots and loved his old home town and all of its people. And, they loved him. He loved the University of Oklahoma, his Sooner teams and his teammates. And he loved his coach and mentor, Bud Wilkinson. Like my son, he embarked on a grand adventure. I never understood through most of my adult life how Darrell could abandon Oklahoma in favor of Texas. It took my son to help me understand. It is, after all, possible to have a heart big enough for many people, places and things to fit inside. It is, after all, possible to treasure the great adventures that life brings and survive the inevitable sorrows. When I finally understood, I began to write Darrell K Royal's story.

PROLOGUE

D ana Xenophone Bible leaned into Darrell Royal and extended his slender, wrinkled pointer finger into Darrell's chest. In a heavy Slavic accent, he whispered, "Dah-role, do NOT go near ze cappy-tole." Bible's admonition resonated with Royal and remained in his head the rest of his life. After all, Bible was the University of Texas's first football coaching icon, having served as head football coach from 1937 to 1946 after back-to-back stints at Texas A&M and Nebraska plus another decade as UT Athletic Director which ended in 1956.

Darrell rocked back in his executive office chair within the bowels of Memorial Stadium and reflected upon how difficult it had been—almost impossible—to follow Bible's advice. The ornate Texas State Capitol stood a few blocks south of the UT campus, informally known as the Forty Acres. The size and stateliness of the capitol spoke to the vast political power—and distasteful meddling—exercised from within its walls. It was now March of 1972, some sixteen years after Bible gave his fatherly advice upon Darrell's hiring as head football coach at UT in the spring of 1957.

It wasn't that things hadn't gone well over the last fifteen seasons. As a coach, Royal's stock was trading at a premium. His Longhorn teams had won Texas's first ever national championship in 1963— and had accomplished the feat in stunning fashion. In 1969, the Longhorns won another national championship in the Game of the Century, defeating Arkansas in Fayetteville with President Nixon in the house. That thrilling season was followed by yet another national championship in 1970. The Longhorns had collected a lot of hardware and Texas pride in a brief amount of time. In fact, words can't adequately express how grateful the Longhorn nation was to "Dah-role." At the highest level, coaching college football requires a constant re-evaluation of both tactical and strategic objectives. As legendary coach Frank "Pop" Ivy once said, "Football is war without casualties." Therefore, a college football coach must examine his position as if he were General Lee at Gettysburg. What are my tactical advantages and disadvantages today? For example, Royal knew that Emory Bellard, his offensive backfield coach, devised the Wishbone offense in the summer of 1968. Various incarnations of that offensive scheme had spread nationwide, most notably to UT's archrival, Oklahoma, as well as to Bear Bryant's Alabama Crimson Tide. Now, in the spring of 1972, Royal had to defend against his own offensive juggernaut every year. His tactical advantage had morphed into a defensive Rubik's cube. Strategically, Royal had successfully navigated the explosion of Texas euphoria following the 1963 season. However, it is axiomatic that money and power migrate to winners. In the state of Texas, that sobering fact takes on unmatched depth and complexity. The Texas culture has as its foundation "Texas exceptionality," which manifests in big oil, power politics, and Longhorn football. Accordingly, strategic coaching decisions weren't entirely Royal's to make. The conflicted coach finessed these matters as best he could.

The 1969 national championship team had been labeled "the last lily white national champions." Certainly the Southwest Conference, of which UT was the flagship institution, had been slow in desegregating its institutions and its intercollegiate athletic programs. Now, in the spring of 1972, that passivity in recruiting black athletes was taking a competitive toll on the Forty Acres. The 1971 Red River Shootout in Dallas featured the two most powerful ground offenses in college football: those of Oklahoma and Texas. Beginning the year before, Oklahoma's offensive coordinator, Barry Switzer, had aggressively recruited and coached black athletes in the nuances of the Wishbone. By 1971, the Oklahoma wishbone was built on blinding speed. It was virtually unstoppable. As a result, the Sooners racked up 435 yards rushing to Texas's 231 in the Red River Shootout. OU halfback Greg Pruitt, a black athlete from Houston's B.C. Elmore High School, rushed for 216 of those yards in only twenty carries, equaling a per carry average of 10.8 yards. The final score was OU forty-eight, Texas twenty-seven, with Pruitt scoring three touchdowns in the game to earn a place in the series record books.

Royal was doing his best to walk on the tightrope of conflicting views about race. At banquets and booster club meetings around the State, he confidently predicted that Texas would always be able to compete and win against the best teams in the country. He had become, by necessity, a devotee of Texas exceptionalism.

Strategically, the uber-rich oil men, the industrialists, and the politicians had to get on board with Royal's decision to recruit black athletes. In the spring of 1972, that was a tall order. There were other troubling matters on campus as well. United States B-52's were carpet bombing Hanoi, the capital city of North Vietnam, as well as Haiphong harbor. These military strikes further inflamed a hyperactive anti-war student faction on the UT campus. Protests had given way to civil disobedience, as was the case around the nation. Students and non-students who were radicalized by Nixon's secret 1970 Cambodian invasion questioned authority—in all its forms. Such unrest perplexed the disciplined, conservative mind of Darrell Royal. He avoided such conflicts. Publicly, he deferred to the higher ups within university administration; privately, he deferred to the aging white male benefactors holding forth in the corporate boardrooms of Houston and Dallas. Doing so day-to-day was a challenge. Royal was, after all, the face of UT athletic glories at a moment in history when a vocal and aggressive student minority wasn't at all interested in those pursuits.

Within walking distance of Royal's office in Memorial Stadium, Frank C. Erwin, Junior was ensconced in the UT Tower as the ultra-powerful chairman of the UT System Board of Regents. In 1969, Erwin had personally intervened at a campus protest undertaken to prevent bulldozing a portion of the greenbelt near Memorial Stadium as part of stadium expansion. Some of the protestors had chained themselves to trees. Erwin, with bullhorn in hand, directed their arrests and prosecution with relish. This incident had occurred just as Darrell was leading the Longhorns to the 1969 national championship that fall. Additionally, the LBJ Presidential Library was in construction a short walk from Memorial Stadium under the watchful eye of Chairman Erwin. Erwin treasured, above all else, his political ties to LBJ and to former Governor John Connally. He believed he was their proxy and could run the University as he saw fit. Under these conditions, the Chairman imposed his will upon every aspect of campus life. Conventional wisdom suggests that having a Presidential Library on campus would be a great source of pride to all; however, the precise location of the library prompted a clash of interests. In 1967, construction for the LBJ Library commenced. Erwin made a shocking suggestion to the Board of Regents. He declared that Memorial Stadium should be demolished in order to make room for parking and other amenities associated with the Library. Erwin believed a new stadium, remote from campus, was in order. In the blink of an eye, Coach Royal was on the phone to the former president. Johnson interceded on Royal's behalf to end such discussions, which led to permanent strain on the relations between Royal and Erwin.

Luring the finest Texas high school football talent to the Forty Acres had traditionally been similar to shooting fish in a barrel. However, by the spring of 1972, recruiting the most talented football prospects had grown as complicated for Royal as deciphering campus anti-war protests. Darrell's assistant coach, Emory Bellard—the father of the Wishbone—left Austin to become head coach at the

Longhorns' instate rival, Texas A&M. Within a matter of weeks, Bellard and his staff had recruited a class of lightning-fast athletes to College Station. Bellard said at the time, "Whatever our freshmen do, they're going to do it in a hurry because they have great speed."

Chuck Fairbanks was not Oklahoma's first choice to replace the popular Jim Mackenzie, who died in the spring of 1967 after a single season as head football coach at OU. Mackenzie had earned his place in the hearts of the Sooner faithful by knocking off Texas for the first time since 1957. The OU search committee pursued Pat James, a tough Alabama protégé of Bear Bryant, who had coached at OU in 1966 before accepting the job as head coach at the University of Cincinnati. James was already preparing for spring practice and couldn't entertain any OU offer that might have been forthcoming. Enter Fairbanks. He was a taciturn man with a no-nonsense demeanor and a right eye that twitched furiously when he got angry. Fairbanks had played football at Michigan State. He'd also labored as an assistant under Coach Bill Yeoman at the University of Houston. Both of these institutions were miles ahead of the Southwest Conference in recruiting outstanding black athletes. Fairbanks understood and was comfortable with integration.

In the spring of 1972, Fairbanks recruited the maximum number of prospects, forty-five, to the Norman campus. Seventeen of them, or thirty-eight percent, were from Texas and twenty-nine percent were black athletes. Among them was Joe Washington from Port Arthur, Texas, plus two stars in the making, brothers Lee Roy and Dewey Selmon from Eufaula, Oklahoma. Strategically, Royal was aware of the revolution going on in college football. His first black football recruit, Julius Whittier, enrolled in 1970 some fourteen years after Oklahoma had enrolled its first black recruit, Prentice Gautt. Progress had been painfully slow. Royal had a grand total of six black athletes out of an approximate total of one-hundred and eighty available players.

Royal's Longhorns produced a sparkling record of ten wins and a single defeat that fall, losing only to Fairbanks' Sooners in the Red River Shootout. Roosevelt Leaks, a fine black running back for the

Longhorns, had performed admirably all season and did so in the game as well. But OU's smothering defense of the Texas version of the Wishbone produced a twenty-seven to nothing Sooner victory.

Winning football games wasn't the only challenge Darrell faced in the fall of 1972. Rather, he was challenged in a very personal way by an unsuspecting critic. Gary Shaw had been a high school standout lineman in Denton, Texas. As such, he was a true believer in all things burnt orange. He had arrived in Austin almost a decade earlier in the fall 1963 and joined his fellow recruits for the many tests of manhood during two-a-days in the sweltering August heat. Over the next four years, Shaw failed to establish himself as a standout performer. In retrospect, however, he must have been radicalized to a degree, like so many hundreds of thousands of college students across America during the same period. Shaw saw no difference between the Army's General Westmoreland in Vietnam and "Daddy D" over at Memorial Stadium. He saw both as frauds. The result was Shaw's 1972 book, *Meat on the Hoof.* There had never been a book quite like it. In it, Shaw delivered his version of Texas football. He laid bare Royal's coaching regimen, replete with instilling fear in its athletes, trampling on human dignity, brutality, academic manipulation, and rampant racism.

Royal tackled the matter following a practice session by acknowledging Shaw's book to his squad. He set about to discredit the messenger, declaring Shaw unstable and disgruntled over his failures on the playing field. Royal was quoted as saying, "I'm not sure I would be happy either as a second-stringer, a dummy holder." Royal's dismissal of Shaw's allegations didn't address the supportive views of several other former UT players, like George Sauer, Junior, an outstanding receiver who went on to star in Super Bowl III and assist Joe Namath to a victory for the New York Jets over the Baltimore Colts.

The shock waves created by *Meat on the Hoof* were followed by a five-part feature story produced by two seasoned reporters for the Associated Press. Authors Robert Heard and Jack Keever painted a grim picture of Texas football as a racist enterprise. The slings and arrows aimed at Royal did little to tarnish his standing with the conservative leadership at UT. After all, the football coach's job was winning—and Royal had certainly achieved that objective. Texas exceptionalism was reflected in the benefactors' unqualified support for Royal. Frank Erwin, however, pressured Royal to recruit black athletes. The tightrope beneath Royal's feet was growing shakier. Erwin, on the other hand, was becoming weary of Royal's failures to follow orders; eventually he sought to have the coach fired. Erwin's efforts failed when Royal's powerful friends came to his defense. The attacks did, however, meant that Royal and the University would immediately and forever after find themselves doing damage control. For the remainder of Royal's career, the University of Texas publicity machine would tout Royal as "representing integrity, respect, and a romantic past."

Marian K Royal, the oldest child of Darrell and Edith Royal, was named after Edith's father, Alfred Marion "Cub" Thomason of Gould, Oklahoma, and Darrell's mother, Katie. Marian was welcomed into the world on July 17, 1945, at the base hospital at what is now known as Macdill Air Force Base in Tampa, Florida. At that time, Darrell was on active duty with the Third Army Air Corps. Marian spent her early years moving with the family from town to town as her dad moved up the coaching ladder. She was twelve years old in the spring of 1957 when she rode in the family sedan from Seattle, Washington, to Austin. Early on, she demonstrated creative talent and fierce independence. Her drawings and sculpted pieces showed promise. Once enrolled at UT, she was drawn to the fine arts. Marian had subsequently met Abraham "Chic" Kazen, a UT law student with an impressive political pedigree. Chic's father, Abraham Kazen, Junior, was a Democratic U.S. Congressman from the Laredo, Texas area. Chic and Marian were married on December 27, 1964, at Saint Austin's Catholic Church. Chic's father interceded to help his son land a federal department job in Washington, D.C. Over the next eight years, two sons, Christian and David, were born. However, by 1972, the marriage had crumbled into a bitter divorce and custody battle over the children. Marian's fierce independence and attraction to the Austin bohemian lifestyle along with her parents' ambivalence toward her in the legal battles left her dazed. In the midst of the family strife, Marian and the boys moved home to Austin where tragedy awaited. One morning, Marian was picking up son Christian from nursery school with toddler David strapped into the front passenger seat. Marian was running late for a lunch date with her former sister-in-law when a UT campus shuttle bus slammed into Marian's car. The accident left her severely injured. Marian passed away on April 11, 1973. Additional agony was visited upon Darrell and Edith when Chic announced he was moving the boys with him to faraway Laredo, where he planned to establish a law practice.

Darrell and Edith grieved in their own personal and markedly different ways. Edith found it difficult to leave the home. Darrell, on the other hand, was out the door each morning to the office or the golf course. To some, Darrell's behavior seemed peculiar. They didn't really know Darrell. He'd felt sorrow and loneliness long before losing his beloved Marian. As a young boy without a mother to nurture him and distant from his father, he had taken to the streets of tiny Hollis, Oklahoma. The Hollis community embraced Darrell as one of their own. He played football, shined shoes at the barber shop, and pitched pennies under the street lamps with his buddies at night. In the spring of 1973, history was simply repeating itself.

THE TOWN

Louella Bryson was walking down Main Street when she bumped into her young friend, Darrell Royal, coming out of the barbershop where he had just finished holding forth at his shoeshine stand. The two visited a few minutes before Maydean Broaddus brushed past the two of them without speaking. Behavior like that was a cardinal sin in Hollis, Oklahoma. Louella leaned over close to Darrell's ear and whispered, "That old bag hasn't spoken to me since she got that high-falutin' job down at J.C. Penney." Of course, there might have been an additional reason why Maydean wasn't acknowledging Louella. Louella was, after all, the town bootlegger.

By 1938, Hollis was surviving the double whammy of the Dust Bowl and the Great Depression as Okies do—with steel resolve and a prayer for rain. The town had lost, however, about a third of its local population; many had little choice but to pack up and head west to California. Farm foreclosures, joblessness, and respiratory ailments from inhaling dust were the root causes of despair. Louella and Darrell were largely unaffected by these tragic circumstances.

Louella had all she needed, thanks to her twice-weekly trips across the Red River into Texas, where she would "invest" in as much cheap whiskey as she could pack into the trunk of her DeSoto. Such an enterprising woman would also acquire moonshine when it was available from some of the farmers in Old Greer County. Inventory and demand were both very good.

Darrell had never known a life of plenty, thus doing without came naturally. He was only fourteen years old, yet everyone from all over town knew him as a budding star on the athletic fields of Hollis and the surrounding towns.

Louella knew everything there was to know about Burley Ray Royal, the widower, his four boys, and the wives who paraded through his bedroom, but not his kitchen. John Steinbeck would publish his novel, *The Grapes of Wrath*, in 1939, telling its iconic story of struggle and sacrifice through the eyes of the members of the Joad family of Oklahoma. The Joads could just as easily have been the Royals. Darrell, at age fourteen, was much like Steinbeck's character, Winfield Joad, the youngest male of the family—"kid-wild and coltish."

Burley Ray Royal had married a local girl, Katie Harmon. They started a family and made do on the various short-term employment opportunities Burley found across town. Burley was an industrious sort, believing in the Christian work ethic of an honest day's work for a full day's pay. Depending upon the times, he was an automobile mechanic, a carpenter, a fence-builder, a hay-baler, and a jailer at the county jail. Burley had to be resourceful. But then, everyone in Harmon County had to be. He had been born in Indian Territory in 1888, a full nineteen years before Oklahoma became a state. Katie Harmon was born a year later, ironically, in what would become Harmon County, Oklahoma.

Burley and Katie produced two daughters, Mahota and Ruby, and four sons. In order of age, they were Ray, Don, Glenn, and Darrell. All were outstanding high-school athletes. It was no surprise, then, that the "Royal boys" were known and embraced by nearly every one of Hollis's 2,400 townspeople. Ray would later become a mechanic in town. Don, a fine high-school football player, would graduate from college and settle down the road at Tipton, Oklahoma, where he would become a coach and teacher. Glenn, a left-handed football passer and baseball pitcher, would also attend college and become a teacher. Thirty years later, when the administration of the University of Texas at Austin took the provocative step of awarding academic tenure to its head football coach, Darrell defended the decision from intense faculty criticism by declaring, "I'm a teacher too, just like the classroom teachers!" In light of his family's background, Darrell must have been speaking with conviction.

The first of Darrell's family tragedies occurred when his mother, Katie, passed away within weeks of his birth. Because Darrell would never know his mother, the family added the letter K to his name. Not an initial. No period. "K" to carry with him the rest of his days.

Burley Ray Royal was a man who had to have a woman in the house. He felt compelled to reconcile this need with his religious nature, which included leading the singing at the Church of Christ. Burley insisted that the new woman in the house, whomever she might be, be married to him. Perhaps. But there was a regrettable thread of consistency to the women passing through the Royal home. They were, more often than not, suffering from a wide variety of illnesses, which left them unable to tend to the household chores. One of Darrell's lifelong friends, Donnie Fox, later remembered visiting the Royal home when Burley called Darrell into the kitchen for a private conversation. The news amounted to yet another announcement of impending marriage. Donnie heard Darrell wail, "Please, Daddy, don't marry another one that's sick!"

Burley's marriages, believed to total five, were so numerous that names, places, and durations had been largely lost to history. Records reflect one other wife, Winnie Wooley Royal, who, fairly or not, is remembered as a hypochondriac who rarely left her bed.

Many often said, "The town raised Darrell Royal." Burley was gone from sunup to sundown, working or looking for work. While working as a jailer, a prisoner grabbed him through the cell bars, whereupon Burley drew his pistol and shot the man in the leg. This surely constituted one of the few times a jailed prisoner has been shot while inside his cell. Because there was little enthusiasm on the part of Burley's wives for cooking and cleaning, the Royal boys were assigned these chores. Louella Bryson felt sorry enough for Darrell that she would occasionally come over to the house to wash the sinkful of dirty dishes while she ordered Darrell outside to play. It was on fall Saturday afternoons in the mid-1930s when, according to Darrell, he would move the RCA Victor radio near the living-room window so he could listen to Oklahoma Sooners' football games while he re-enacted the game in the yard. Years later, he recalled hearing the OU band play "Boomer Sooner" and dreaming the band was playing just for him.

As Darrell matured, so did his remarkable athletic talent. Despite being a shade under five foot ten and weighing 150 pounds, he was muscular, lacking a single ounce of fat. His jet-black hair and broad grin suggested a future as a charismatic adult. He could play any sport with skill and confidence.

A tall water tower stood squarely in the middle of town. It provided water pressure for the town's citizens, but it also served as an informal line of demarcation between east and west Hollis. When Darrell was in the eighth grade, he played little league baseball for the east team, sponsored by the Kiwanis Club. Donnie Fox played for the west team, sponsored by the Rotary Club. Donnie later recalled one particularly intense game between the cross-town rivals when Darrell was pitching for his team. The plate umpire, a surly and rotund fellow, reduced the strike zone to the size of a postage stamp. Darrell complained loud enough for everyone in the stands to hear. Finally the umpire yelled back, "You can kiss my ass!" Darrell instinctively and instantly replied, "Well, you'll have to mark a spot because you look like all ass to me!" The formidable wit that Darrell would exhibit all his life was already manifesting itself.

Difficulties at home continued. One of Darrell's stepmothers resented having boys to deal with, taking particular umbrage with young Darrell. One afternoon, knowing that Darrell had saved up his shoe-shining money and had bought a new, leather baseball glove, she turned on the yard hose and soaked the glove as it lay in the grass. "That'll teach you not to leave your things lying out in the yard," she bellowed. Nothing, however, would alter Darrell's love affair with sports. The playing fields gave him comfort and a sense of belonging. Even as an eighth grader, he played on the junior-varsity football team composed of boys one or two years older.

In the spring of 1940, Burley could not ignore the incessant siren call to join the mass migration of God's children to the promised land of California. The parched, drought-stricken Harmon County had left him weary and broke. Darrell had just completed his freshman year at Hollis High School. Once again, the young man was traumatized. Of course, he didn't want to leave his support group: his friends, Doctor Will Husband, and Dean Wild, his football coach. Burley argued, "There's work out there for all of us, son. We've gotta eat!"

Just as WPA photographers so vividly captured in their black-and-white photos, families just like the Royals loaded up everything their old cars could carry and headed west to the land of plenty. All the excess weight on the old balloon tires led to many flat tires along the way. Darrell became proficient with the patch kit and the hand pump. The Royals landed in Porterville, California, due north of Bakersfield in the San Joaquin Valley. Steinbeck described those days in the *Grapes of Wrath* through the eyes of Tom Joad: "Okie used to mean you was from Oklahoma. Now it means you're a dirty son-of-a-bitch. Okie means you're scum. Don't mean nothing itself, it's the way they say it." Like his industrious father, Darrell held a variety of jobs as a common laborer over the summer of 1940, painting figs hastening them to ripen, and pouring concrete.

Some said war was coming. People on the streets of Porterville talked about what they'd heard on the radio about the Germans' *blitzkrieg* of London. Despite that distant threat, Darrell looked forward to enrolling at Porterville High so he could play football and make some friends. More importantly, he wanted to earn respect. After a few August practices, the coaching staff at Porterville informed Darrell he was "too light" for varsity play and directed him to the junior-varsity squad. Darrell was devastated. Because he was fiercely competitive and understood the game as well as his coaches, he knew he could contribute mightily. The coaches' decision was really another form of discrimination. He was the Okie. The migrant laborer. He didn't measure up. Burley heard his son's pleas and felt the sting of rejection himself. Burley had received a handwritten letter from Coach Wild back in Hollis that was orchestrated by Doctor Will. It said that if Darrell were allowed to return to Hollis, he could live with his Grandma Harmon and the community would take care of him. Almost overnight, Darrell packed his belongings in a rigged up Victrola box and hitchhiked across country to Hollis. He was home.

Doctor Will Husband could have appeared in the television series Gunsmoke playing the part of a frontier doctor. Indeed, that's precisely what Doctor Will was. He made house calls. He delivered babies in farmhouses. He set broken bones, sutured cuts, and diagnosed life-threatening illnesses. Moreover, he was dearly loved by the citizens of Harmon County. Doctor Will was trusted so much that no matter what he wanted to do, he was fully supported around town. In many ways, Doctor Will loved his life. He knew the life-blood of the community he served was high school athletics. Thus he adopted the red-and-white-clad Hollis Tigers. Doctor Will looked after the players' and coaches' best interests in every way. He watched the Royal boys grow into outstanding high school athletes. He knew everything about their difficult home life. In fact, he had delivered Darrell. It was no surprise, then, that he found a way to encourage Burley Royal to allow Darrell to return home. Darrell had multiple part-time jobs waiting on him there. After school, he was to sweep out the high school gym. After that, he was to race down to Cecil Sumpter's barber shop to man his shoeshine stand. Donnie Fox once said, "Some days I'd sweep out the gym for Darrell so he could get on down to the dozen pairs of shoes left at his shoeshine stand." Yet there was another hurdle to Darrell's settling into his familiar routine at Hollis High School. Because he transferred from Porterville High, he was ineligible to play for Hollis during his sophomore season. The 1940 Tigers were going to be very good. Coach Wild needed Darrell's special talent to contend for a state title. The away games posed the biggest threat to victory. Coach Wild and Doctor Will concocted a plan to address the challenge. Darrell played away games under an assumed name—Bill Husband. Bill was Doctor Will's young son—and not an athlete. No one would ever challenge the name "Husband" on this matter nor any other. The ruse was successful.

Darrell fell right back into his friendships with his teammates, including Donnie Fox and Ted Owens. Fox recalls that running around town with Darrell had its benefits: "I always liked going to eat with Darrell down at Bess Felder's Café. Eating alongside Darrell on stools at the counter meant Bess would speak with us and more importantly, that Bess would put more meat in our stew." Down at Sumpter's barbershop, the men of the business community left their church shoes for Darrell to shine before Sunday services. Business was so good that Darrell had a key to the shop so he could get down there early on Sundays to catch up. Every Sunday morning about nine o'clock, Doctor Will would stop in to pick up his black brogans. A shine cost 50 cents. And every Sunday morning without fail, Doctor Will would hand Darrell a folded 20 dollar bill.

To say that the Hollis townspeople took their high school football seriously would be an understatement. Leon Manley was a hulking kid who excelled on the offensive line. Leon Heath was a muscular youngster who could run with the football and was almost impossible to tackle. Ted Owens was a speedy defensive specialist, and Donnie Fox manned the tight end and defensive end positions. The local harvest of players was truly outstanding. But the team could be further improved. Doctor Will's avocation outside of his medical practice was recruiting football players for the Hollis Tigers. Hollis is located in the far southwest corner of Oklahoma, less than five miles from the Texas state line. At that time, the governing body of Texas high school athletics had a regulation that no high school student over the age of eighteen could participate in high school athletics. On the other hand, in Oklahoma, the regulation stated that participation was allowed through age 21. Doctor Will saw an opportunity. He scoured the west Texas towns of Childress, Vernon, and Quanah, among others, for talented athletes that were ineligible to play in Texas but still eligible in Oklahoma. Academic standing was irrelevant. For Doctor Will, locating quality athletes was the easy part. The bigger challenge was arranging for the families of these mercenaries to relocate to Hollis, finding them a place to live, and finding jobs for the heads of household. Doctor Will's labors produced a bounty of quality athletes. Hollis was a powerhouse in high school football at a time when there were no divisions among high schools of vastly different sizes. Thus when playoff time rolled around, Hollis was pitted against much larger towns. Doctor Will educated Darrell on team building. Today, the Hollis Tigers play in Doctor Will Husband Stadium—on Darrell K Royal Field.

Life at Grandma Harmon's house was not exciting. The only available entertainment was listening to the radio which Grandma always tuned to ministers preaching hell, fire, and brimstone, or the gospel music hour. Down on Main Street, however, things were more interesting.

Public schools were segregated in Hollis just as they were everywhere in the 1940s. Black students attended their own school across town from Hollis High. As a result, Darrell never played an athletic contest against black athletes in any sport while he was in high school. That didn't mean he didn't pitch pennies and shoot dice with young black men of his age and economic standing. He certainly did. Darrell wasn't incorrigible. He didn't look for trouble. But if trouble found him, he wouldn't walk away from it. His brand of mettle, strength, and agility were packed into a sliver of tendon and gristle weighing 150 pounds.

Donnie Fox recalls an episode involving himself, Darrell, and two black acquaintances from the streets, Rodney and Sermon. None of them had access to transportation except for Donnie. He could count on getting his grandfather's Ford pickup keys most every evening. Donnie's parents were divorced and he lived with his grandparents. Compared with other local boys, Donnie lived quite comfortably. One evening when Donnie got keys to the pickup, he and Darrell discovered Grandpa's shotgun and heavy hunting coat and hat behind the seats of the pickup. Always the alpha male in the truck, Darrell devised a prank.

Donnie and Darrell spotted Rodney and Sermon hanging out downtown under a street light. On Darrell's word, Donnie gunned the old pickup past the boys and headed for Fairmount Cemetery a few blocks away. There, Darrell pulled on the heavy coat and pulled the hat down nearly over his ears. He slid a shell into the chamber of the shotgun and climbed to the top of the old wooden windmill at the edge of the cemetery. Meanwhile, Donnie returned to town to pick up Rodney and Sermon, while Darrell waited in the darkness of the cemetery. Rodney and Sermon jumped at the chance to ride in the pickup. Donnie headed for the cemetery. "Just ridin' around," he told his passengers. Donnie parked in the cemetery near the base of the old windmill. He suggested they all get out to pee. The passengers readily agreed. (It's amazing what a nighttime visit to a cemetery will do to a boy's bladder.) Once the two acquaintances were clear of the pickup and Donnie had locked the door behind them, BOOM! Rodney and Sermon shrieked and bolted back to the pickup only to find the doors locked. "Let us in! Let us in," they screamed. Donnie yelled back, "You better run!" They certainly did—all the way back to town. Darrell climbed down from the windmill where his laughter rose on the breeze, across the headstones, plowed fields, and into the night.

Despite the coming of World War II, more great times lay ahead for Darrell. During the 1941 football season, the Oklahoma Sooners—Darrell's favorite team—continued to dominate his dreams. One Saturday a local man, Petey Pickens, a relative of future oil billionaire T. Boone Pickens, offered to drive Darrell to the Oklahoma–Nebraska football game in Norman. Petey let Darrell ride but charged him a dollar for gas.

By the fall of 1942, Darrell was a senior in high school and was leading the Hollis Tigers as their star quarterback and defensive back. He was an outstanding punter as well. Hollis finished the season undefeated. When they were voted fourth in the final state poll by a panel of sportswriters, the town was indignant. Since the Enid Plainsmen had been voted state champion and Enid was a much larger town than Hollis, Coach Wild challenged Enid to a game. Enid, of course, declined. It was the first time Darrell had lost out on a championship. It would not, however, be the last.

TAIL GUNNER

Donnie Fox was shooting baskets through the hoop nailed to his grandpa's garage, still wearing his church clothes. It was a Sunday afternoon not unlike any other in Hollis, Oklahoma. The sun was out warming the fields and sending the frost scurrying away. Grandpa appeared at the back door and called out, "Sonny boy, you need to come in." Donnie took two more jump shots and then climbed the three stairs into the house where Grandpa and Grandma met him in the kitchen. "The Japanese bombed Pearl Harbor. It's on the radio." Donnie could tell by the concern in his grandfather's voice that this was serious business. He didn't know then where Pearl Harbor was, but he learned soon enough. The United States Pacific fleet had been largely destroyed by Japanese planes appearing out of the western sun, flying low over the bay. Life was about to change for every American high school kid. At Hollis High, teachers explained what they knew about the disaster and explained patiently that the war would require everyone to sacrifice—and many to put on the uniform. Within a few months, they established Altus Air Field some twenty-five miles east of Hollis to train fly boys for the Army Air Corps. Conversation about it down at Bess Felder's Café set Darrell Royal to dreaming about adventures and glories to be won on faraway battlefields.

The two local movie theaters began to show Movietone news-reels of Allied action in Europe and North Africa. It seemed heroes were being made weekly. Darrell, Donnie, and others at Hollis High were itching to enlist. They would need to turn eighteen and finish high school first. The year 1942 lay ahead, which meant one more year of high school football. But after Christmas of 1942, Darrell couldn't wait any longer. He told Grandma Harmon that he had to go. Like grandmothers all over the country, she tearfully consented. Darrell caught a ride to Lawton to enlist. His entry physical revealed that he had water on his right knee, brought on by the rough-and-tumble football season that just passed. Doctor Will drained the knee and Darrell was good to go. President Roosevelt and Prime Minister Churchill dominated the radio broadcasts, speaking of the defense of freedom at home and abroad. They succeeded in establishing a sense of the "noble cause" young men and women were called to pursue. It seemed to Darrell that there was honor and glory in waging war against Hitler. It never occurred to Darrell that there was any danger associated with military service.

Life in Hollis before was insulated, safe, and slow-moving. Those aspects of life were now taking on new meaning for everyone. There was a sense of urgency in everything. In the winter of 1942, Darrell encountered a young woman at the local roller skating rink that caught his eye.

Edith Thomason was born during an unusually severe early winter blizzard in her family's remote farmhouse on October 27, 1925. She was the first born of Marion "Cub" Thomason and Miss Addie Mae. Three brothers would follow her. The blizzard into which she was born would never really end, as she spent her life caring first for her younger brothers, then Darrell, then her own children. Her nurturing but stoic nature was a necessity, not a choice. During those few weeks before Darrell left for basic training, he couldn't see Edith unless he could find transportation to the Thomason place

20

located near the banks of the Salt Fork River. Edith didn't attend Hollis High School. Instead, she attended Gould School, a few miles east of Hollis. Darrell could count on his buddy Donnie Fox to lend him the family Studebaker so he could make the trip north to court Edith. Years later Darrell declared, "If it hadn't been for Donnie's Studebaker, I don't think Edith and I would have gotten married."

Edith's Grandpa Thomason was a first rate frontier cotton farmer. He knew soils, planting seasons, phases of the moon, and prayers that produced rain. He had learned the farmer's life in Jack County, Texas, southeast of Wichita Falls. But when the Oklahoma Territory was opened to settlement, he and his brother had already ridden their horses into the territory north of the Red River and followed a tributary northwest until they spotted the land that would become the Thomason place. The brothers staked their claim to 500 acres on the south side of the Salt Fork River in what would become Old Greer County. They divided the acreage and went to work making lives for their families there. Once, on a trip to Lawton in a horse-drawn wagon to buy supplies, Grandpa Thomason took his family and infant son Marion Thomason along. By happenstance, the family met the legendary Comanche leader, Quanah Parker, at the general store in Lawton. When the great Indian warrior peered into the baby blanket in Ms. Thomason's arms, he grinned and declared, "He look like bear cub!" Hence and forevermore, the baby Marion was known as "Cub" Thomason.

Over the succeeding decades, Cub Thomason learned how to manage as a frontier farmer. When hard times hit in the 1930's, Grandpa Thomason's brother and family joined the migration to California, leaving Grandpa and Cub to operate his farm—and fire up his moonshine still if they saw fit. When Cub came of age and married Miss Addie Mae, the couple moved into his departed uncle's farmhouse. Miss Addie Mae set about to make a home of the old place. The thick dust covering the floors and windowsills had to be scrubbed away. The Dust Bowl had certainly come to Old Greer County. The nearest community was Gould, twelve miles south over treacherous sandy roads. There was no electricity. A privy stood out back. Cub took on the challenge just as his country neighbors came to expect. This good and decent man was a fine cotton farmer and a trusted friend. By the time Edith was born and had grown to be a toddler, Cub landed a job working for President Roosevelt's Workers Progress Administration (WPA), which brought work to millions during the Depression years. Miss Addie Mae taught first grade at Central View School while Cub also worked at the school as a maintenance man. As the years passed, Edith took on more and more of the household chores associated with her three ornery brothers. Attending school meant walking to the nearest county road to catch the school bus. Edith recalls a loving family life during these challenging Depression-era times. She was a good student and even won an oratory contest held among area schools in Mangum, Oklahoma.

By the time Darrell spotted Edith at the Hollis roller skating rink, she had blossomed into a lovely young woman. She had beautiful, long, dark hair, full lips, and a petite figure. By the time Darrell left for basic flight training at Davis-Mothan Air Field in Arizona, Darrell and Edith were in love. Darrell's sense of urgency in joining the fight against the Nazis required him to leave before his high school graduation. He received his diploma after the war when he returned to Hollis. In succeeding months, Darrell was transferred to Miami, Florida where he took up residence in the venerable Kent Hotel (today an art deco treasure). The hotel, like others along Ocean Drive, had been expropriated by the government for use as military housing. Darrell loved those days. Wearing his uniform among the Floridians on Miami Beach prompted a splendid short-term adventure. Meanwhile, his letters to Edith expressed his love and hope for their future. Edith said, "I walked the two miles to the mailbox every day to see if I got a letter."

Later, when Darrell was transferred to Oklahoma City's Will Rogers Field, Edith packed a bag and her high school diploma and took the bus to Oklahoma City intent upon finding a job and spending time with her sweetheart. She landed a job almost immediately on a production line waterproofing airmen's flight suits at Tinker Air Field.

When Darrell was able to secure a pass to leave the base, he'd come downtown to meet his sweetheart. Occasionally they'd walk to the Municipal Auditorium to listen to the latest country and western musicians play. Darrell's interest in guitar picking would last a lifetime. More often they would sit on the front steps of Edith's modest apartment building and talk. On one such starry evening, Darrell squeezed Edith's hand and said, "Let's get married." Doing so required a bit of planning. Neither owned a car. But the First Methodist Church was walking distance from Edith's apartment. At the first opportunity, Darrell walked down to the church and booked an appointment with the minister to perform the marriage. When Darrell next earned weekend leave, the new Mr. and Mrs. Royal took the bus from Oklahoma City to Altus, where they spent their wedding night at an old hotel on the Jackson County square. The next morning, Darrell's faithful friend Donnie Fox and his wife Melba arrived in the Studebaker to pick them up and transport them to the Thomason place. While Donnie and Melba waited in the car, Darrell and Edith lugged their suitcases up the steps and knocked on the door. Cub Thomason opened it and Edith said, "Daddy, we got married!" To Donnie's relief, Cub replied, "Well, come on in."

The newlyweds found a studio apartment in a big white clapboard apartment house run by a "mean old lady". No matter. Darrell and Edith were oblivious to the outside world, save the news from Europe's western front. Darrell took his assignment as a B-24 tail gunner seriously. How could he not? It was serious business to be hanging in a glass bubble off the tail of a vibrating propeller-driven bomber loaded with ordnance fending off fighter attacks. Just to be selected for the assignment meant Darrell had the "right stuff".

While stationed at Will Rogers Field, Darrell used his free time to play basketball for the Will Rogers Eagles and to play baseball with his mates. Darrell's unusual skills and competitive spirit did not go unnoticed by the base commander. He heard the glowing reports from coaches. Such athletes provided esprit de corps to young boys going to war. Thus, when Darrell developed acute appendicitis and required surgery, the brass found a replacement for his spot on the

B-24 crew. It wasn't long after his recovery that he received orders for transfer to Tampa Air Field, which later became MacDill Air Force Base. Tens of thousands of young enlisted men were being moved around the country by train. Many of these soldiers were newlyweds, just like Darrell and Edith. The complicated psychology of young men wishing to wed before deployment and the girls' equally urgent pleas to tie the knot were ever present during the war years. Riding a troop train from Oklahoma City to Tampa proved especially daunting for Edith. She was four months pregnant. The crowded, smoky passenger cars were not air-conditioned. The GIs opened all the windows to get a breath of fresh air, which was welcome enough despite that the trip through the Deep South brought them only hot, humid breeze. Edith remembers, "The train stopped in Birmingham for us to stretch our legs and eat. I'll never forget that tiny café. And those grits and flies."

Once in Tampa, the couple found a room available to rent from Sue Lou Bedingfield. "Mother Sue Lou" took an uncomfortable Edith under her wing as the pregnancy continued. On July 17, 1945, Edith gave birth to a baby girl at the base hospital. After a difficult delivery, Edith and Darrell cradled the infant in their arms and agreed on the name Marion for the child, after Marion "Cub" Thomason. Years later, the child changed the spelling of her name to Marian.

Darrell instantly became a valued member of the Third Army Air Corps Gremlins football team and earned the nickname, "The Duke." Military teams of the day were coached by other military men with coaching backgrounds and were provided full equipment. They arranged games against other base teams whenever possible. Word spread about outstanding players through letters, post cards, and official communications among base officers. The football coaches at Iowa Pre-Flight, Jim Tatum and Bud Wilkinson, were learning a new offense called the Split-T from early strategist Don Faurot. These military men took their football as seriously as they did their military service. Accordingly, the coaches kept a list of every outstanding player in the military just in case a transfer could be arranged. Darrell Royal would have been on any such list. Another member of the Gremlins team in Tampa was Charlie Trippi, the great University of Georgia athlete who returned to Athens after the war to become a 1946 All-American and the number one draft pick in the 1945 draft even before his military discharge. Another Gremlin teammate was Huel Hamm. Hamm had been a fine University of Oklahoma player from 1940 to 1942. He was married and had a child, so the Hamms socialized with the Royals. There was much in common between the couples. Edith recalls that "Huel was a smoker, so we sold our rationing stamps to Huel so he could buy cigarettes." Unquestionably, Hamm influenced Darrell to consider going to OU after the war.

After the Allied victory over the Axis powers in September of 1945, Darrell, Edith, and Marion returned to Hollis and took up residence in yet another rental place. Special eligibility rules were enacted by the National Collegiate Athletic Association to accommodate servicemen returning from the war. For example, there were no prohibitions against tryouts, awarding scholarships, or age limitations. It wasn't long before Darrell started receiving dozens of letters addressed simply to Darrell Royal, Hollis, Oklahoma.

CRIMSON AND CREAM

Eastern universities had been playing a primitive version of football for a couple of decades before a confident young lad, John A. Harts, declared, "Let's get up a football team!" to the fellows down at Bud Risinger's Barber Shop in Norman. The year was 1895. The University of Oklahoma consisted of a single red brick building standing in a row of elm saplings on a broad expanse of plain. This was the Oklahoma Territory.

Meanwhile, across the Red River to the south lay the former Republic of Texas, a vast landscape of diverse demographics and interests. The Republic had lasted only a decade, 1836 to 1846, before its leaders lobbied the U.S. Congress for statehood. In 1846, their pleas became a reality. The first vestige of Texas exceptionalism coupled with the use of a singular word, "big," were woven into the culture and have proven durable for the last 160 years. Texas was, in fact, big. It was by far the biggest state in area at the time. A mere fourteen years after statehood, in 1860, the state legislature joined the Deep South states in seceding from the union. Its young men joined the Confederate States of America army and were shipped off in regiments to the distant killing fields of Franklin, Nashville, and Tupelo. In some instances, the Confederates were led by veterans of the Mexican-American War which had secured Texas's independence. The Civil War's horrors of death and destruction never really scarred Texas. Its remoteness and its vastness rendered it of little strategic value to either side. The young men in gray had served valiantly in the "Lost Cause," leaving only a residual notion of defiance for the survivors to pass on as their enduring legacy. In fact, relocation to Texas appealed to many Confederate veterans who wanted to forget and make a fresh start.

The next 80 years accelerated Texas's development, which came about as a direct result of migration, the discovery of oil, and the energizing effects of two world wars. Meanwhile, the Oklahoma Territory achieved statehood much later, in 1907. It experienced its own unusual birth beginning with the Land Run of 1889. No one had ever seen anything like it and never would again. Common folks itching to own land of their own propelled themselves across the dusty prairies in clouds of dust and hope. Those scoundrels who slipped in under the cover of darkness to stake an early claim were labeled "Sooners." That can-do spirit—that reckless optimism—was woven into the fabric of these seekers. Thus they built for themselves and for future generations a spiritual resolve that could and did withstand most anything. From the Dust Bowl and the Great Depression they emerged bloodied but unbowed.

The game of football was much later in coming to the OU campus. Oklahoma and Texas, the two states' flagship universities, first played each other at the turn of the century in 1900. The game was in Austin. A ragtag group of Oklahoma Rough Riders climbed on a train in Norman for the long trek south. One player brought along several bottles of milk from the family milk cow for the team members to share on the trip. Oklahoma's coach was a professor—a Harvard man, V. L. Parrington—who would later win the Pulitzer Prize for his academic work. Parrington's charges lost the game twenty-eight to two. Over the next four years, the two squads played each other in Austin because there were no suitable facilities in Norman. In an event that reflected the hard-scrabble enterprise of football, a young UT graduate, Mark McMahan, played with an independent group against the Oklahoma squad in Dallas at the State Fair on October 15, 1902. McMahan's squad was variously called the Dallas Athletic Club or the Texas and Pacific Railroad team, depending on what entity was paying the team's expenses at the moment. The Rough Riders arrived full of grit and ready to play but sadly without a coach. The Texas indies won that game eleven to six. Later that evening, McMahan found his way to the Oklahoma team hotel and offered to coach the team. They struck a suitable bargain. Coach McMahan manned his post for the rest of 1902 and all of 1903 and earned enough money to pay off his law school debts and move to Durant, Oklahoma to practice law. This turn of events led to McMahan posing for the 1902 Oklahoma team photo wearing his conspicuous block "T" sweater. However, in 1905, the contest was in Oklahoma City and for the first time ever, Oklahoma won the game by a paltry score of two to nothing with a rowdy group of supporters cheering them on.

The old-style game and the growing intensity of the annual Oklahoma–Texas matchup would continue to evolve with changing rules and huge fan bases that would eventually follow the teams to road games. Additionally, the Allied victory over the Axis powers in 1945 had some unexpected consequences. New technology allowed coaches to communicate with each other by telephone line between the sidelines and the press box. Film cameras mounted high in the stands could record the games for future analysis. In Norman, a wealthy oil man, Lloyd Noble from Ardmore, was serving as a university regent and exhibiting bravado that verged on empire building. In a regents' meeting with OU President George L. Cross in the days before the Japanese surrender, Noble suggested that OU could become an instant football juggernaut by bringing hundreds of discharged, battle-hardened military veterans to the OU campus for tryouts. To be ruthlessly efficient, Noble said, the administration needed to hire a new football coach with ties to the military teams of recent years. These mature vets were all immediately eligible, even as transfers from other universities. OU Athletic Director Jap Haskell, who had just returned from military service himself, noted that he had become acquainted with a tightly-wound, competitive fellow named Jim Tatum who had coached at the University of North Carolina before going into the service. Tatum had later coached the Iowa Pre-Flight Seahawks and also at the Pensacola Air Station. The regents authorized Haskell to solicit a meeting with Tatum.

The notes Tatum kept in a spiral notebook contained a trove of information on outstanding service team players he'd observed or heard about. Another young naval officer, Charles Burnham "Bud" Wilkinson, was equally diligent in recordkeeping and player evaluation. Tatum's notebook had an entry about an outstanding player on the Third Army Air Corps Gremlins team who had Oklahoma roots. His name was Darrell Royal.

After VJ Day and tens of thousands of young men receiving their discharge papers, veterans headed home to see their families and sweethearts. Letters arrived by general delivery to Darrell Royal, of Hollis, Oklahoma. Other letters were forwarded to him from his former post in Tampa. They came from coaches from Southern California, Georgia, Florida, Oklahoma, and other universities. There is no evidence that Royal was recruited by the University of Texas. In any event, Darrell wanted to live out his boyhood dream of wearing the crimson and cream of the Oklahoma Sooners. Darrell happily accepted paid visits to other campuses, pocketing the travel money and hitchhiking instead. These savings later allowed the Royals to buy an old Chevrolet from OU teammate Buddy Burris. Having accepted OU's scholarship offer, they packed up and got on the bus for Norman where extraordinary events awaited.

It wasn't as if other major universities weren't searching high and low for returning veterans with athletic skills and valued maturity. They were. Coach Jim Tatum approached everything with the reckless abandon that was unique and a bit unsettling. When Tatum interviewed with the OU regents and President Cross, he had insisted on bringing Bud Wilkinson along as well. The two of them emerged from a low-slung Hudson at the OU Fieldhouse where the coaches' offices were located. Bronko McGugan, the "All-American substitute," was there. Bronko said, "Bud made the best impression right off the bat. He had a regal bearing. Coach Tatum seemed brash and driven to the point of recklessness." The OU Regents shared Bronko's views. During a break for lunch, the regents discussed whether it would be prudent to offer the head job to Wilkinson. President Cross nixed the idea, saying "It would not be appropriate to interview a candidate for the coaching position and then offer it to his proposed assistant. And if the assistant accepted the head job, he wouldn't have demonstrated the character we're looking for in a coach." The regents and Cross elected to offer the job to Tatum on the condition that he bring Wilkinson along with him. The last remaining hurdle was that Wilkinson had not planned on going into coaching. He planned on joining his father's mortgage banking business in Minneapolis. Everything about Bud's personality, polish, and technical skills supported doing just that. The erratic Tatum leaned on Bud hard, saying, "Just come for one year so I can land this job. Then you can go back to Minneapolis." Bud reluctantly agreed.

During the 1946 summer spectacle unfolding on the practice fields at the University of Oklahoma, some 300 to 400 young men arrived by bus, train, airplane, car, and thumb. Tatum and Wilkinson checked their names off as fellows reported to the coaches' offices. Some were total unknowns who had simply heard about the open tryouts. The coaches welcomed them. A Darwinian theory of survival of the fittest was enacted during those sweltering summer afternoons. Rudimentary drills determined agility, stamina, and most importantly, toughness. Leon Manley, the Hollis native and future University of Texas assistant coach said later, "I'd never seen so many suitcases coming and going in my life." There was no conviviality in the whole undertaking. It was more like basic training in that regard. The washouts were sent packing. Those that remained formed a circle so Tatum could address them all. There were so many players in the enormous circle that guys on one side couldn't make out who was on the other side. The coaches organized the squad by position and diligently recorded the exceptional talents in their notebooks.

Players who had the right stuff had somehow made it to Norman from all over the country.

The modern era of football was born in the fall of 1946. A giddy nation, fresh off a war victory, had produced what would later be called "The Greatest Generation." Hundreds of thousands of members of the Greatest Generation were home now, intent on going to college on the GI Bill, starting businesses, buying bungalows, and producing babies at such a rate that it created "the Baby Boom." Some genuine war heroes were coaching and playing college football. Coach Tatum took this opportunity to feverishly recruit those fellows who had been outstanding college players at other institutions before the war. One such example was Jack Mitchell from Arkansas City, Kansas. Jack had been a fine high school player at Ark City and was recruited to Austin in 1941 by Coach Dana X. Bible. Mitchell was tall, handsome, with tousled jet black hair and charisma to match. He was a born leader. When he stepped off the troop train in Ark City in the spring of 1946, Jim Tatum was waiting for him. So it was that a promising Texas Longhorn quarterback became an Oklahoma Sooner right there on the train platform. When he was asked fifty years later why he transferred, Jack replied through his infectious grin, "Texas already had a guy named Bobby Layne and I wanted to play quarterback."

From the very beginning of fall practice in 1946, Jack Mitchell and Darrell Royal competed as quarterbacks. Mitchell was three years older than Royal but that didn't mean they were anything less than fierce competitors on the practice field. Mitchell was the better runner. Royal was the better passer. Each was masterful running the precision Oklahoma Split-T. In the fall of 1946 and every succeeding fall through 1948, Mitchell would start at quarterback and Royal would be moved to halfback, defensive back, and punter. Royal was an artful dodger at every position. Moreover, he was an acute student of the game. He had a knack for grasping the nuances of all aspects of the Sooners' playbook.

Edith was pregnant once again. She tended to baby Marian and maintained quiet in the rented duplex while Darrell studied for his business classes and turned his attention to his football playbook. Darrell and Edith moved into a big drafty duplex located at the corner of Flood and Lindsay streets, a few blocks west of the OU campus. A Jewish couple, Fran and Gershon Frankel, lived on the opposite side of the duplex. Gershon's parents owned a kosher grocery store in Shawnee, Oklahoma. Life was fresh and new for these young married couples. A door between the two duplex units was left open during the day so that the mothers could "hear the babies." Darrell took some of his meals with his teammates at the training table. The lessons from rationing during the Great Depression, the Dust Bowl, and World War II never left Edith. She didn't throw anything away. Fifty years later, she could still find little scraps of paper containing her handwritten monthly household budgets.

Meanwhile, on the practice fields, the Oklahoma Sooners prepared for a monumental challenge—playing the Army Cadets on the banks of the Hudson River at West Point, New York before a crowd that included President Harry Truman. Additionally, Army featured the nation's two most celebrated football heroes—Doc Blanchard ("Mr. Inside") and Glenn Davis ("Mr. Outside"). Moreover, Army had won national championships in 1944 and 1945 and would do so again in 1946. Mr. Inside won the Heisman Trophy in 1945, followed by Mr. Outside in 1946. One had to wonder why Oklahoma would even schedule such contests. There were explanations.

Anything involving OU Coach Jim Tatum involved elements of intrigue. In this instance, Doc Blanchard had played football at the University of North Carolina in the fall of 1942 in part because Coach Tatum's cousin was Blanchard's mother. The Oklahoma–Army matchup produced stories which are now the stuff of legend. In the end, OU lost the game twenty-one to seven. In Austin, the University of Texas was preparing to play its last season under future College Hall of Fame coach Dana X. Bible. Texas was ranked number one in the country going into the season. On October 12, 1946, Texas and Oklahoma met once again on the floor of the Cotton Bowl. Texas was heavily favored. Star Longhorn quarterback Bobby Layne attempted a series record thirty-one passes and completed eighteen to book yet another series record. Layne, Tom Landry, and OU's Darrell Royal all threw interceptions. The final score was Texas twenty, OU thirteen.

Blair Cherry was a fine high school coach at Amarillo High School who got passed over for the UT head coaching job in 1937 in favor of the more experienced Dana X. Bible. However, Bible invited Cherry to join his coaching staff. Bible came to rely on Cherry and groomed Cherry to succeed him. Cherry served as offensive coordinator at Texas from 1937 through 1946 and then followed through on Bible's plans by succeeding Bible as head coach. Bible moved into the Athletic Director's position.

Edith Royal gave birth to Sammy Mack Royal in February of 1947 at Norman Hospital where she was attended by the OU team physician. Darrell remained focused on school and football. Math and all matters analytical came easy for him. In a stunning turn of events, the University of Oklahoma football program experienced its own changing of the guard. After OU's Gator Bowl victory over North Carolina State in OU's first bowl appearance ever, the impulsive Coach Tatum chartered a flight for his squad to visit Havana, Cuba as a reward. Additionally, Tatum was holding secret negotiations with University of Maryland officials about accepting the head coaching position there. When OU President George Cross caught wind of Tatum's activities, he changed his plans and flew to the Gator Bowl, not to speak with Coach Tatum but to speak with Bud Wilkinson. Cross wanted Tatum to leave and Wilkinson to take over as head coach. They struck a bargain. Upon the team's return to Norman, the OU administration learned that Tatum had spent the entire Athletic Department budget for the academic year. With that news, both Tatum and Athletic Director Jap Haskell were summarily fired. With that, Wilkinson's career plans took an abrupt turn. He knew how good the returning team in 1947 would be. The ultimate strategist and planner set about to prepare for the upcoming season while Blair Cherry did the same in Austin.

Jack Sisco grew up in Waco, Texas and attended Waco High where he was a fine multi-sport athlete. He went on to play football at Baylor as a lineman. With him, the Baylor Bears won the 1924 Southwest Conference title. Sisco pursued a coaching career and eventually became head football coach at North Texas State Teachers College (now the University of North Texas). He completed his career there in 1941 when World War II began. Somewhere along the line, Sisco began refereeing football games to make extra money. That experience credentialed him to officiate college games. Jack Sisco died in 1983 at 79 near Corsicana, Texas, but not before becoming a footnote to the Oklahoma–Texas rivalry.

Darrell Royal had become a precious commodity to the Oklahoma Sooners. The annual competition with Jack Mitchell began again in the spring of 1947 and again Royal was moved to halfback by the time September rolled around. Darrell continued doing all of the punting and some placekicking, and eventually earned himself a national reputation as punter. He had enough control of the ball that he could regularly punt it out of bounds inside the 5-yard line, a feat called "hitting the coffin corner." One evening after practice, dusk was settling in on the practice field and Coach Wilkinson was leaving to walk home. He noticed Darrell was still on Owen Field with a sack of footballs, punting them one after another. Coach Wilkinson called out to Darrell, "Hey, you need to go on home to your wife and kids. You've practiced enough for the day." Darrell replied, "I know Coach, but I want to find out what I can do when I'm tired."

Meanwhile, 350 miles south of Norman, Bobby Layne was planning for the October 11 match up with his archrivals from Norman. Texas came into the game ranked third in the nation while OU was ranked number fifteen. The contest was hard fought but took a bizarre turn when referee Jack Sisco made a series of calls that uniformly benefited the Longhorns. The game appeared to be turning in OU's favor when, in the fourth quarter, Darrell Royal intercepted a Bobby Layne aerial to halt a Texas drive at the OU thirty-eight yard line. Enter Sisco. His penalty flag for roughing the passer against OU nullified Royal's interception, reversed possession of the ball from Oklahoma to Texas, and advanced the ball fifteen yards to the OU twenty-three yard line. Sisco wasn't done. In any event, Texas scored once more and the game was essentially over. The final score was Texas thirty-four, Oklahoma fourteen. Multiple melees broke out in the stands. A storm of bottles, cans, hip flasks, and seat cushions hailed on to the turf. Sisco was whisked away in a police car. Years later, Jack Sisco moved to Shawnee, Oklahoma and applied for membership in the elite private Sooner booster group, The Touchdown Club. His application was denied.

By spring practice of 1948, Norman's Sooners had reason for optimism. Those mature young war veterans were using Coach Wilkinson's method of repetition, repetition, and then more repetition, and were running the Split-T with the precision of a Swiss watch. The competition knew this as well. Sportswriters in Texas and the southwest in general complained that Oklahoma had built its juggernaut with mercenaries—athletes who had never visited Norman or even Oklahoma before agreeing to play for the Sooners. Some of these published complaints were, of course, fed to the media by coaching staffs at other universities. Wilkinson's methods of addressing these complaints were subtle but somewhat effective at the time. For example, Texas transfer Jack Mitchell was listed as being from Ponca City, Oklahoma, although he'd never lived there. It was a fact, however, that Mitchell was the child of divorced parents and that his father did live in Ponca City. Bobby Layne left UT for the Chicago Bears. The Longhorns were formidable just the same. OU's annual spring quarterback carousel featured Jack Mitchell and Darrell Royal as usual. The trio was now joined by Okmulgee, Oklahoma native Claude Arnold. Claude was only three months younger than Darrell but he'd played football while serving in the military in California. Claude was biding his time. Remarkably, the tiny county seat town of Hollis, Oklahoma, had produced four outstanding football players on the OU roster. Besides Royal, there was offensive tackle Leon Manley (Royal's assistant coach in the Austin days to come), Leon Heath, a bruising fullback who would earn the nickname, Mule Train, and J. W. Cole, yet another tough-as-nails lineman.

The 1948 OU–Texas game was played on October 9, 1948, before the largest crowd ever to see a football game in the southwest—70,000 plus spectators. Texas was pegged as the favorite by two touchdowns. The charismatic Jack Mitchell would say years later about the 1948 Sooners, "When they blew that whistle, it was like a house afire." By October, Oklahoma had recovered from the wounds of losing the season opener to Santa Clara in San Francisco. The Sooners would not lose again for 31 games. Onlookers in the Cotton Bowl watched as OU posted a fourteen to nothing lead behind the running of Hollis boys, Royal and Heath. Royal's splendid punting put Texas in a hole more than once. However, Texas narrowed the score with the help of quarterback Paul Campbell's passing prowess. OU led Texas fourteen to seven at that point. Four minutes later, Mule Train Heath bolted free for a sixty-eight yard run to the Texas twelve yard line. George "Junior" Thomas scored on the next play. OU appeared to have a comfortable twenty to seven lead at that point. The feeling of security lasted less than three minutes in real time when UT track star and kick returner, Perry Samuels, took the ensuing kickoff and accelerated. Samuels was a blur once he cleared the first wave of tacklers. But Darrell Royal gave chase and managed to catch Samuels from behind at the OU twenty yard line. Tom Landry scored from the six yard line to cap off the Longhorn drive. With that conversion, the game score tightened to twenty to fourteen. Sooner fans were hyperventilating. They hadn't beaten Texas in nine years. That year, their luck changed. Twenty to fourteen was the final score. The Golden Hat, awarded annually to the victors, was hauled across the Red River for the first time ever. Next, Oklahoma had to prepare to play in the Sugar Bowl, where they took on the University of North Carolina and their star running back, Charlie "Choo Choo" Justice. Choo Choo and his Tar Heel mates disposed of Texas by a score of thirty-four to six earlier in the season. In Oklahoma's preparation for the Sugar Bowl game, defensive back Darrell Royal was charged with stopping Justice—a challenging assignment. With a suffocating defensive performance by Royal and OU linebacker Myrle Greathouse, OU defeated the Tar Heels in a low-scoring affair, fourteen to seven. Jack Mitchell was named Most Valuable Player of that game, which was also his last college appearance.

The Sooners had finished the season 10–1. Darrell was proud enough of his performance against the Tar Heels that he carried the metal canister containing the game film and an old projector around in the back seat of his car. He wanted to watch the game anytime he wanted. And he wanted other friends and family to see it as well. One thing was certain. He would be the starting quarterback for the Oklahoma Sooners in the fall of 1949. For Darrell K Royal, it was never too early to start preparing.

THE UNDEFEATED

S ome football historians believe the 1949 Oklahoma Sooners were the best team in the country that year. The Sooners only lost one game during the previous season, in their home opener to Santa Clara played in San Francisco. They finished the season 10–1 and defeated North Carolina in the Sugar Bowl.

Darrell and Edith Royal harbor golden memories of the fall of 1949. Darrell had become a master operator of the Oklahoma Split-T offensive formation. He was a fine passer even though Coach Wilkinson rarely allowed him to demonstrate it. During his coaching career, Darrell would later come to embrace Wilkinson's disdain for the pass. He said, "When you pass, three things can happen and two of them are bad." Wilkinson's Split-T caught the attention of coaches across the country. When these coaches came to Norman in the spring and summer of 1949 in order to learn more about the nuances of the formation, Wilkinson would simply tell them, "Meet Darrell Royal down at the practice field in an hour and he'll show you what we do." These referrals placed Darrell in the company of some of the finest coaches in the country. The visitors were impressed with his knowledge and instructional methods. Occasionally after practice, Darrell, Edith, and the kids would walk from the stadium down to Campus Corner and order malts at Liberty Drug. When "Picture Day" for the press rolled around, Edith dressed her two young ones up and took them over to the practice field. There are some treasured photos of Darrell in game uniform with son Mack running alongside him wearing his All-American sweater. Marian, the adorable daughter, looked exactly like Shirley Temple, with her frilly dress and ringlets in her hair, hugging her daddy's neck.

A handsome young man hung around practice quite often that fall. Edith recalls, "You could tell he wanted to be out there in uniform more than anything." Darrell didn't pay much attention. He had his hands full with the seemingly endless repetition that Wilkinson believed was necessary to refine the offense. In fact, Darrell had quite a lot in common with the handsome stranger. Both Darrell and the young man had grown up in households without their birth mothers. Both spent most of their time hanging out down on the streets of their communities, making mischief and telling jokes. Neither boy had money to buy a hamburger but for two cents, for example, the grill man at the Norman hamburger joint would run a bun around the hot grill and soak up the burger juice, turning the bun a toasty brown and making a tasty treat. In the young stranger's case, he lived a few blocks from Campus Corner with his brothers, dad, and evil stepmother, whom he simply called "Red." In order to get away from Red, the young man had already dropped out of high school and gone to California to find a job, similar to the way that Darrell had ventured out. Years later, in 1957, Darrell and Edith went to a movie theatre in Austin to watch a new release called *Sayonara* starring Marlon Brando. In the middle of the movie, Darrell leaned over to Edith and whispered, "That guy up there looks just like that kid that used to hang around practice in Norman." They waited for the credits to roll at the end of the movie, at which point Darrell exclaimed, "Why, that IS that kid from Norman!" Today, a life-sized statue of that "kid" dressed for his most famous role as Maverick stands on Norman's Main Street. The kid's name was James Garner.

The 1949 pre-season Associated Press rankings listed Notre Dame as number one, Army number two, Oklahoma number three and Texas number twelve. Both the Sooners and Longhorns had romped over their September opponents and arrived in Dallas undefeated. The Cotton Bowl Stadium expanded during the second postwar construction boom and now featured a new upper deck on the east side. Stadium capacity had grown to 75,504. The game settled into a fierce seesaw battle with the Sooners' Darrell Royal, Leon Heath, Junior Thomas, and Jim Owens powering the offense. The Longhorns' Randy Clay sparked the Longhorns with his running and placekicking. Texas quarterback Paul Campbell had success running the "Statue of Liberty" play, a fake pass and handoff to a circling halfback, and with it kept the Longhorns' offense moving. In the fourth quarter, Royal tossed to end Jim Owens in the corner of the end zone for a touchdown and padded the Sooners' lead to twenty to seven. The Longhorns scrambled back and scored late, leaving them losing by a final score of twenty to fourteen, the same final as the prior year. Texas finished the season a disappointing 6–4, while OU ran around and through each opponent and finished 10–0. It was only logical that number two Oklahoma should be matched against number one Notre Dame in a bowl game. However, this was not the case. Notre Dame would not participate in postseason bowl games until years later.

Accordingly, OU was once again tabbed for the Sugar Bowl and was matched against a mediocre LSU Bengal Tiger squad. Most of the excitement took place a few days before the game. The Sooners were practicing in Biloxi, Mississippi at a football field that had a couple of wooden storage sheds across the field from the stands. Coach Wilkinson was in the process of installing a drop-back passing package and some defensive wrinkles as well. During practice, Doctor C. B. McDonald from Oklahoma City—who was among the Sooner entourage—noticed a glint of light coming from under a blanket stretched on a wire between two of the storage buildings. Doctor McDonald and a uniformed security officer proceeded to investigate. A photographer tagged along when the group surprised a man with binoculars and a note pad hiding under the blanket. The photographer snapped a classic photo of Walter Lee "Piggy" Barnes, a former LSU offensive lineman, as he was accosted and the tools of his trade seized. When the area papers published the picture of "Piggy the Spy," Wilkinson cried foul. When Darrell read the story in the paper accompanied by the photo, he showed it to Edith over breakfast and said, "Why, that guy Piggy looks like a condom salesman!" The incident would not be Darrell's last practice spying episode.

The 1949 spying incident may have spurred a public outcry because of the striking photograph. Otherwise, the episode should not have been surprising. Spying has always been a tactic of war in the corporate world and in sports. The Central Intelligence Agency calls it "intelligence gathering." If there are ethical lines that should not be crossed in high stakes college football, they are at best ill-defined.

During the 1940s, a trend in awarding trophies emerged in college football. Consider the context of AP voting in the war years and immediately afterwards:

1943	Notre Dame national champion
	Angelo Bertelli, Notre Dame quarterback, Heisman Trophy
1944	Army national champion
1945	Army national champion
	Glenn Davis, Army halfback, Heisman Trophy
1946	Notre Dame national champion; (Army Helms Foundation national champion)
	Doc Blanchard, Army fullback, Heisman Trophy
1947	Notre Dame national champion
	Johnny Lujack, Notre Dame quarterback, Heisman Trophy
1949	Notre Dame national champion
	Leon Hart, Notre Dame end, Heisman Trophy

To be sure, Notre Dame and Army were powerhouses in the 1940s, as was continually noted in New York and Chicago newspapers. Their 1946 matchup was dubbed by some as "The Game of the Century."

The metrics are telling. Over the war years of 1943 through 1949, Notre Dame won four AP national championships for fifty-seven percent of the titles awarded during the period. After 1949 and over the next sixty-five years, Notre Dame won an additional four national championships for six percent of the titles awarded during the period. During the same period from 1943 to 1949, Notre Dame produced three Heisman Trophy winners for forty-three percent of the awards given during that period. Over the next sixty-five years, Notre Dame produced four Heisman Trophy winners for six percent of the awards given during the period.

Consider Army. Over the seven years from 1943 to 1949, Army won two AP national championships (plus one Helms Foundation national championship, not included here), for twenty-nine percent of the national championships awarded by AP during that period. Over the next sixty five years, Army has never won another AP national championship. In the same years between 1943 and 1949, Army produced two Heisman Trophy winners for a total of twenty-nine percent of the Heisman Trophies awarded during that period. Within the next sixty five years, Army produced one additional Heisman Trophy winner, Pete Dawkins, in 1958. That's 0.015% of the awards given during that sixty five year period.

It might be said of these numbers that things have changed since then. Indeed they have. During the seven year control period from 1943 to 1949, Notre Dame and Army enjoyed special advantages in garnering AP votes. First, Notre Dame was located in Chicago, a major metropolitan area with high circulation newspapers and sportswriters. More importantly, Notre Dame enjoyed a national fan base among Catholics and a national network of Catholic high schools grooming future Notre Dame stars.

Army was also located in a major metropolitan area, New York. They too enjoyed all of the benefits of high circulation newspapers.

More importantly, the United States Military Academy enjoyed the largest fan base possible—that of a nation grateful for their service.

None of the nation's leading sportswriters had ever seen Oklahoma play. The Sooner program had yet to distinguish itself.

Darrell Royal's 1949 Sooners may have been the best college team in the country that year. What we know for certain is that for the second time in his life, Darrell quarterbacked an undefeated football team—the 1942 Hollis Tigers and the 1949 Oklahoma Sooners—and neither had been rewarded as champions.

Royal Family Collection

CLIMBING THE LADDER

E dward R. Murrow, Uncle Miltie, Brown vs. Board of Education, and the Red Scare all entered American homes in black and white images during the fifties. The advent of television gave a face to newsmakers, entertainers, politicians, and football coaches. Actually, the television had been in the making for nearly a century by the time CBS made the leap from radio to images issuing from a mahogany box. Edward R. Murrow was the first newsman most Americans came to know with his program, *See It Now*. The Red Scare engineered by Wisconsin junior Senator Joseph McCarthy riveted the public but validated democracy when Murrow courageously called out McCarthy as a fraud. Milton Berle became a household name by transforming his old vaudeville stage act into a hilarious slapstick comedy on the Texaco Star Hour. For the first time, film brought the Korean War into the homes of millions of Americans.

College football games appeared on local television on the east coast as early as 1939. At the time, their transmission was viewed as a novelty. Home televisions were a decade or more away and were only available to those who could afford the luxury. However, by 1950 a few universities contracted for the regional broadcast of their football games. Notre Dame University was among the first of these, contracting with the Dumont Television Network to broadcast into the Chicago market. Today, Notre Dame remains highly protective of its own network deal with NBC to broadcast all Fighting Irish games nationwide.

It would be an understatement to say that television changed the lives of Americans. It is significant to note, however, how TV began to impact sports. Its effects went far beyond merely broadcasting games. It made celebrities of young broadcasters like Walter Cronkite and Curt Gowdy. Player interviews, for which many of the young men were unprepared, were followed by studio coaches' shows, for which most all coaches were unprepared.

During Darrell Royal's senior year at Oklahoma, 1949–1950, there was extensive print coverage and radio coverage of live football action, but no television coverage. That suited Darrell fine because he was self-conscious about his public speaking. He was certainly capable enough. He just lacked training and experience. For Charles Burnham "Bud" Wilkinson, however, poise, polish, and articulation came naturally. Bud came from a banking family in Minneapolis. His father, C. B., was a polished Wall Street type. C.B. knew how to pitch a business deal. Further, Bud attended graduate school at Syracuse University, where he studied English literature and also made time to assist the football coach, Ossie Solem. Bud was a young man with a path to success laid out before him. He had no intention of pursuing the crudities of coaching football, even despite being an All-American in the sport at the University of Minnesota. Mere happenstance led Bud Wilkinson to Norman, Oklahoma and to building a football dynasty.

After the Sooners' all-victorious season of 1949, Wilkinson was chosen as Coach of the Year by the National Football Coaches Association on January 12, 1950. The New York sportswriters who covered events at the coaches' convention had never seen someone like Wilkinson. Bud wore tailored suits, polished lace ups, and a neatly-folded white handkerchief in the breast pocket of his suit. His polish led Bud to become the standard against which college coaches would be judged. In 1946, less than one percent of American homes had television. By 1954, when Wilkinson's football juggernaut was at full throttle, fifty-five percent of homes had television. Bud was laying the foundation for the Oklahoma Sooners to ascend to the national stage.

There is no clear answer to why Darrell Royal didn't take his business degree from OU and go into the thriving oil business like so many of his peers. His Hollis friend and teammate, Ted Owens, played basketball at OU while Royal was quickly becoming a football star. Ted writes in his autobiography, *At the Hang-Up*, that becoming a teacher was an honorable profession in Hollis. Indeed, that was what attracted him to coaching; he coached the University of Kansas Jayhawks basketball team for years. Whatever Darrell could have chosen to do, he would likely have been successful. He worked hard at everything he took on. More importantly, he was a "people person" with a ready handshake and a big smile. People liked him.

In the 1920s, "Tonto" Coleman was a fine athlete at Abilene Christian University in Abilene, Texas. After serving in the Army Air Corps during WWII (where he may have become acquainted with Darrell Royal), Tonto became Abilene Christian's football coach. There, he served through the 1949 season before leaving to take a job as assistant coach at the University of Florida. Before departing Abilene, Tonto contacted Darrell to take over the head coaching job there despite that Darrell hadn't coached a single day at that point. Darrell recognized his lack of experience and declined the offer. A few weeks later, Darrell accepted an offer to coach football at El Reno High School, some thirty miles northwest of Norman. Before Darrell could get fitted for his coaches' cleats, Beattie Feathers, head coach at North Carolina State, called to offer him a spot on his coaching staff. This was more in line with Darrell's reasoning. He knew that to insure his progress up the ladder in the coaching profession, he needed experience as an assistant. He managed to get his Sooner teammate Wade Walker, who was also an All-American, a job as line coach on Feathers' staff. Feathers had no doubt paid attention to Darrell's play at defensive back during the Gator Bowl on January 1, 1947 in his freshman year. In the bowl game, Oklahoma's first ever, the Sooners dominated the Wolfpack thirty-four to thirteen. While Beattie Feathers had been an outstanding college football player himself at Tennessee and in the NFL, he did not succeed in the coaching ranks. His 1948 and 1949 seasons were losing ones. Thus he knew he had to make major changes quickly. Whatever Darrell and Wade Walker were able to contribute was not enough to salvage Feathers' sinking ship. NC State finished with a 1950 record of 5–4–1, and Coach Feathers was out of a job. Halfway across the country, the Oklahoma Sooners won ten straight games and nipped Texas fourteen to thirteen on their way to OU's first national championship. They had Darrell's quarterback understudy, Claude Arnold, controlling the precision Split-T. Coach Wilkinson's sterling reputation together with outstanding organization and disciplined play had validated Oklahoma as a football powerhouse. It's impossible to know what went through Darrell's mind when he read the Sunday sports pages that autumn. He had led the 1949 Sooners to an undefeated season and then watched as Notre Dame was voted national champion. This may have steeled his resolve for the days ahead and certainly reinforced a belief that being a great football team isn't always enough.

Darrell received a telephone call from Coach John "Buddy" Brothers at Tulsa University. Brothers had heard good things about Darrell's coaching talent and offered him a position coaching offense for the Golden Hurricane. Darrell did his homework and knew that Brothers had been successful at Tulsa over the previous five years. Under his leadership, they won the Missouri Valley Conference championship in 1946, 1947, and 1950. Additionally, Brothers was honored as Missouri Valley Coach of the Year after the 1950 season. Within a matter of days, Darrell, Edith, and the kids arrived in Tulsa. Then Bud Wilkinson called. Darrell's mentor explained that he had an opening for an offensive coach and wanted Darrell to come home. Wilkinson had just coached his team to a national championship.

Darrell told Bud he would think it over. In the end, Darrell declined Bud's offer. His reason, he said, was that Buddy Brothers wouldn't let him out of his contract with the Golden Hurricane. A more plausible explanation is that Darrell didn't want to coach under a living legend. He found a reasonable excuse that he knew Wilkinson had to accept. Moving up the coaching ladder had never been a problem for Darrell. However, this was different.

Darrell undertook his tasks at Tulsa with the intensity he always brought to his performances as a player and as a coach. Change was underway among the coaching staff at the University of Texas as well. Blair Cherry had finished his fourth season in the fall of 1950, by sweeping to the Southwest Conference championship and finishing the season ranked number three in the AP poll. He took the Horns to the Cotton Bowl where they lost to Tennessee, twenty to fourteen. Cherry posted two top-five finishes. Despite it all, Cherry was under fire from fans and the media. The explanation for their ire was simple enough. Cherry had lost to Oklahoma three years in a row in 1948, 1949, and again in 1950. To make matters worse, young Bud Wilkinson had just led his charges to its first national championship, something Texas had yet to achieve. Cherry had heard enough complaints. He resigned from his position at UT and never coached football again. Texas scrambled to find a replacement, finally settling on a staff assistant, Ed Price. Price began his tenure in the fall 1951 and remained head football coach through the 1956 season. By that time, Oklahoma had won three national championships.

Edith Thomason Royal had married a football coach. As such, she probably never completely unpacked her suitcase. Better to be ready when the next move came. Murray Warmath had just accepted the job as head football coach at Mississippi State and was assembling his staff. In the spring, 1951, Edith was on her way to the Deep South, as Darrell joined the new staff for the Mississippi State Bulldogs.

The revolution that was unfolding at the time in other aspects of American life included matters of race. "Separate but equal" had governed public education since the Plessy v. Ferguson Supreme Court decision of 1896. Segregation was the law. In 1948, President

Truman issued an Executive Order that mandated integration of the armed forces. Congressional action regarding this policy change would never have gotten through. Senators and congressmen from the Solid South would never have allowed it. By the beginning of the Korean War in late 1950, there was little tangible integration of the military. It took the Korean War and the effectiveness and heroism of all-black units in combat to spur incremental integration. In July of 1951, three years after Truman's executive order, the U.S. Army announced its plan to desegregate.

Southern whites were seething at the intrusion of government into their culture. Northern states, removed from Jim Crow laws in the Deep South, had already allowed blacks entry into all manner of public institutions, including colleges and universities. The predictable result was that northern universities embraced black athletes on their athletics teams while southern states still shunned the idea. Coach Merrill Green recalls, "I was at Texas Tech then and the subject of recruiting blacks just didn't come up." Indeed.

In the winter of 1950, Oklahoma A&M Athletic Director Henry Iba was searching for a new coach for his football team. He telephoned OU Athletic Director Bud Wilkinson. Iba wanted a recommendation from Bud. After a cursory review of prospective candidates, Bud suggested that Iba hire Jennings B. "Ears" Whitworth. Whitworth played at the University of Alabama and had subsequently been an assistant there as well as at the University of Georgia. Ears was a southerner who was comfortable with the existing segregationist culture. Iba hired Whitworth, after which Wilkinson mentioned to his closest associates, "I recommended Ears. I knew he wasn't worth a damn." What is beyond debate, however, is that Coach Whitworth instigated one of the most cowardly, intentional, racially-motivated physical assaults in college football history.

Johnny Bright entered his senior season at Drake University with great promise. He was considered a candidate for the Heisman Trophy. He was, halfway through the season of 1951, leading the nation in both rushing and total offense. As a member of the Missouri Valley Conference, the Drake Bulldogs traveled to Stillwater, Oklahoma to play conference foe, Oklahoma A&M. The Stillwater newspapers and the campus paper labeled Bright a "marked man." Stillwater was a segregationist town. Newsmen from Des Moines were there with their cameras. They'd read the stories. Accordingly, they trained their cameras on Bright. True to the newspaper columns, Johnny Bright was knocked unconscious three times over the first seven minutes of the game. A&M defensive tackle Wilbanks Smith had been assigned the ugly task of immobilizing Bright. Wilbanks had even practiced using his forearm shiver to the face. The final forearm shiver from Smith broke Bright's jaw, effectively ending Bright's participation for the day. One Des Moines photographer captured Wilbanks's blow in sequential shots. Those photos made national news. Because neither A&M nor the Missouri Valley Conference would take disciplinary action against Coach Whitworth or his squad, Drake University and Bradley University both withdrew from the conference. The Johnny Bright incident led to modest rules changes and a mandate from the NCAA for more helmet protection. Such changes were beside the point. The Johnny Bright incident occurred because bigots supervising every aspect of the football game allowed it to happen. Coaches, officials, and administrators were ultimately responsible for the cowardly act. Darrell Royal undoubtedly read about the incident. After all, he was coaching at Tulsa University, another member of the Missouri Valley Conference. Wilbanks Smith had grown up in Mangum, Oklahoma, a community thirty miles from Royal's home town of Hollis. Royal loved the game of football and may have been disgusted—but probably not surprised—when he learned of the incident.

As for Johnny Bright, a horrified nation honored him as an All-American. He finished fifth in the vote for Heisman Trophy and was awarded the Swede Nelson Sportsmanship Award. Finally, in 2005, over fifty years after the incident, Oklahoma State University issued a formal letter of apology to Drake University through its president. Johnny had passed away by that time, but today, Drake University plays its home football games on Bright Field. As for Ears

Whitworth, he left Oklahoma A&M after the 1954 season to become head coach of the University of Alabama Crimson Tide.

Darrell and Edith packed up once again and headed for the historic Mississippi county seat of Starkville. Edith remembers pulling into town for the first time. "It looked like a scene out of *Gone with the Wind*. All the old buildings . . . all the old homes. We liked it." Edith was certainly correct about the visible aspects of Starkville, Mississippi in the spring of 1952. The old Cotton District was visually appealing but concealed its embrace of slavery. Its Greek revival architecture combined with classical and Victorian designs were reminiscent of the French Quarter in New Orleans. Edith certainly would not have known that behind some of those doors were members of an active klavern of the Ku Klux Klan. The Royals moved into a lovely home. It was the finest living Edith had ever experienced. She accepted a referral for an African-American maid and nanny, Annie, who immediately began helping Edith adjust to her new surroundings. It felt safe there. In fact, it was. Every morning, Edith would drive over to Annie's modest family home to pick her up for work. In no time at all, Annie was a part of the Royals' extended family.

At Mississippi State, Darrell found an institution devoid of football tradition. Coach "Slick" Morton, Murray Warmath's predecessor, had lost every game in 1949 save one. That one was a tie. The 1950 and 1951 seasons were somewhat better. Both seasons ended with identical 4–5–0 records. And yet, there was an undercurrent of frustration in Starkville. "Slick" had never beaten the University of Mississippi, informally known as "Ole Miss." Mississippi State was the land grant university. It was previously known as Mississippi A&M. Up the road to the northwest, in Oxford, stood the state's flagship university, Ole Miss. It had the law school and the medical school. It also educated the elite children from Jackson, Mobile, and Natchez. The University's athletic teams were the Rebels, and proudly displayed the Confederate battle flag. Competitive feelings ran deep between the two state universities.

Murray Warmath was from Tennessee, where he played football at the University of Tennessee. Adjusting to the burdens and benefits of southern living were no stretch at all for the Warmath family. Warmath and his youthful coaching staff went to work. Once again, Darrell arranged for his old teammate, Wade Walker, to join the staff as offensive line coach. Recruiting was conducted very differently in those days. Assistant coaches spent most Friday fall evenings watching high school football games and schmoozing with the star players and their coaches before hurrying back to Starkville to prepare for Saturday's home contest. Prime recruits from places like Gloster, Tupelo, and Meridian received loads of letters on fancy stationery and home phone calls as well. The MSU Bulldogs were an all-white team. No African-American would enroll there until 1965.

During the fall of 1952, Darrell was assigned to work with the offensive backs. Repetition. Precision. Discipline. The winning concepts Darrell had embraced as a college player were instilled in his charges. Results were mixed. The Bulldogs finished the season 5–4–0. Coach Warmath made the best of it and declared that they'd posted a winning season, albeit barely. Warmath couldn't excuse the fact that his squad had lost to the Rebels from Ole Miss.

In a stunning turn of events, Darrell tendered his resignation after the 1952 season in order to accept his first head coaching position— of the Edmonton Eskimos in the Canadian Football League. One only had to examine a map of Canada to wonder what was going through Darrell's head. He was leaving the Deep South where football reigned supreme to go to a remote outpost where hockey reigned supreme. In fact, Edmonton was known as the "Most Northerly City in North America," populated by perhaps 200,000 citizens at the time. The Edmonton Eskimos football team was organized just a few years before, in 1949, after Annis Stukus—of the locally famous "Stukus Brothers"—agreed to organize a team. The Stukus brothers played Canadian football with a relish seldom seen in those parts. In a stroke of luck, the University of Alberta was discontinuing its college football program and donated all of its uniforms and equipment to the Eskimos. Since the University's mascot was the Golden Bears, the pre-owned uniforms were green and gold. Hence the Edmonton Eskimos' colors have always been green and gold. Coach Stukus remained their coach for three years before departing to organize a team in the more seasonable province of British Columbia.

It wasn't geography that bothered Coach Royal. Rather, it was the lack of talent, discipline, and motivation among his squad men. In late July of 1952, he only had a few weeks before the season opener to instill in his squad the intangibles that Royal had learned back home in Hollis and later in Norman. Team scrimmages were nightmarish. Linemen mushed into pileups like they were involved in a rugby scrum. If nothing else, Darrell was an intense competitor. What he was witnessing was painful. It was time to rethink his strategy.

The old farm boy from Royal's hometown had always been a bearish lineman, first at Hollis and then at OU. Despite being almost two years younger than Darrell, Leon Manley had come to Norman the same summer in 1946. Years later, Bud Wilkinson said that "Leon Manley was the finest tackle I ever had at OU." Strangely, Manley didn't make All Big Six in any of his seasons of 1947, 1948, or 1949. Manley never made All-American. Part of the reason may have been that two other Sooner linemen received the accolades. Guard Buddy Burris was a three-time All-American in 1948, 1949, and 1950, while tackle Wade Walker was an All-American in 1949. However, Manley was drafted by the Green Bay Packers in 1950. He spent two years with the Packers before receiving a call from his lifelong friend, Darrell. Manley listened to Darrell's frustrations and agreed to travel to Edmonton immediately. Royal told a friend, "Leon will show 'em how it's done or kill 'em, one way or the other." With Manley on his way, Darrell felt energized. Incredibly, he talked Claude Arnold— quarterback of the 1950 national champions—into packing his bags for Edmonton. Frankie Anderson, the All-American end on the same national championship team, showed up too. Darrell had enlisted a tough offensive lineman, a fine passer, and a splendid receiver. But the best was yet to come. Billy Vessels, the 1952 Heisman Trophy winner, agreed to come to Edmonton. These young men cared about Darrell and they cared about each other. Four of the best college football players of their generation were now Edmonton Eskimos, if only for a brief time.

During Darrell Royal's single season with the Eskimos, Billy Vessels was awarded the league's Outstanding Player Award. During that season, Vessels led the Western Division of the CFL with 926 yards rushing plus an impressive number of pass receptions and interceptions while playing defense. Vessels was simply playing a game with which the other young men were not familiar. The same could also be said about the Hollis farm boy, Leon Manley. He was added to the CFL All-Star team of 1953.

Meanwhile, change was afoot back in Starkville, Mississippi. Head Coach Murray Warmath was offered the head coaching job at the University of Minnesota. The coaching merry-go-round continued with Warmath moving to Minnesota where he would remain for eighteen years. Darrell accepted the job as head coach of Mississippi State, where he would not remain nearly as long.

The prior experience Darrell had at MSU in 1952 provided him a jump start in preparing for the 1954 season. Wade Walker stayed on the coaching staff to assist with line coaching duties. Walker was admired for his deep, slow, southern drawl and congenial demeanor. His players liked him. A former teammate remembers Wade's practice field work habits. "Wade moved awful slow at practice. He didn't care for warm-ups and always said, "I get warm enough just practicing." The MSU coaching staff was required to devote Longhorns to advance the Bulldogs' cause. That's the only way Coach Royal knew how to do it. The 1954 squad finished with a record of 6–4, as did the 1955 squad. In neither year did they defeat their arch rival, Ole Miss.

Darrell and Wade paid attention to the successes enjoyed by their mentor in Norman, Bud Wilkinson. The 1954 Sooners finished the season undefeated. The following year, 1955, the Sooners again finished undefeated and were crowned national champions for the second time in the preceding five years.

Out in the Pacific Northwest, the University of Washington was struggling with a scandal within its athletic department. It was discovered that donor money was being pumped into a secret account and was being used to benefit recruits and enrolled student-athletes. The head football coach, John Cherberg, was summarily fired, as was the athletic director. The new athletic director, George Briggs, offered the head coaching job to three of the young Turks of the college game: Michigan State's Duffy Daugherty, Texas A&M's Bear Bryant, and Oklahoma's Bud Wilkinson. Each of them turned down the job but Wilkinson recommended Darrell Royal. Coach Royal agreed to a four-year contract at 17,000 dollars per year, which was considered a hefty sum for coaching football at that time. With Darrell's support, Wade Walker replaced him as head coach at Mississippi State. The Royal family was off again, this time to Seattle.

For the first time in his coaching career, Darrell would have several African-Americans on his football team. While in Edmonton, he coached only one black player, Rollie Myles. Desegregation in the United States was still very much a contested issue. But Darrell and Edith were always able to adapt to changing conditions. Winning football games and managing the household were their primary objectives in those days.

Paul "Bear" Bryant arrived from the University of Kentucky to take over an all-white Texas A&M team in the spring of 1954. At the time, A&M was a proud all-male military school. Bryant perceived a softness in his football players which was inconsistent with the military bravado that the Aggies had come to stand for over the years. Bryant's harshness prompted many players to quit the team on the spot. The remaining eighty or so team members were transported by bus with the coaching staff to the small town of Junction, Texas. The rigors they endured over the next ten days were sufficiently brutal for a book and TV movie to be made about them. Practice began each day before dawn and continued until dark. Drought conditions had left the ground as hard as concrete. Goatheads and burrs made the practice area unfit for use. Bryant didn't allow water breaks. Dozens of players quit from exhaustion or disgust. After Bryant's camp concluded, he had roughly thirty-five survivors remaining—barely enough to scrimmage. The book, *Junction Boys*, and the movie of the same name exposed the barbarity of those days and glorified those that held up under the physical and mental abuse. Word got around the college football circles about those days at Junction. Other coaches who respected Bryant now were not so sure. Is this how you build a football team? If there had been black athletes on the team in 1954, would they have tolerated Junction? Probably not. The revolution hadn't reached Junction just yet.

Darrell Royal always held firm to simple principles: don't follow a coaching legend and don't follow rich tradition. In the winter of 1956—unlike the University of Oklahoma—the University of Texas had neither. For Darrell Royal, opportunity was about to come knocking.

THE EYES OF TEXAS

Fifty-five percent. That's the winning percentage Darrell Royal posted in three years as a college head coach. His prior head coaching jobs were efforts at rebuilding—just the way Darrell liked it. The University of Texas was one such rebuilding project. The decade from 1946-1956 had brought no joy to the Forty Acres. Dana X. Bible coached the Old Style Game and the succeeding coaches couldn't adapt to the demands of modern play. They also lacked the charisma that Texas exceptionalism demanded.

In their book, *The Triple Package*, Yale law professors Amy Chua and Jed Rubenfeld make provocative claims about the secrets of success. According to the authors, there are three secrets. The first is a superiority complex. A person with the courage to compete and succeed must have confidence in his own exceptionality. Pride. Strength of will that is manifested in word and deed. Second, self-doubt. A successful person is privately fearful that he or she is not good enough. Finally, a successful person must have impulse control.

Restraint. Wisdom for discerning which opportunities to seize upon and which to abandon.

Dana X. Bible wasn't thinking about these character traits when he sat down with Darrell Royal for an interview in 1957. Still, one can imagine that Bible may somehow have recognized such traits in the young man from Oklahoma.

Royal accepted the position as head football coach at Texas with relish. The job met all the criteria Royal was looking for. He believed he could build a proud, successful program at Texas. He could measure his successes annually against those of his mentor, Bud Wilkinson. Finally, if successful at his tasks, he could build a legacy that would be unparalleled in Texas football history. Such were the ambitions of the new coach of the Longhorns. He understood that as a young, unproven coach, he would be mercilessly scrutinized. He had seen this happen with Bud Wilkinson back in 1947 up through 1949. Back then, the media speculated that Bud was too young and too inexperienced. Bud knew that he needed to win quickly to silence the naysayers. If Royal had studied the political landscape at UT in 1957, he might have assessed the job as dangerously unstable. Wealthy businessmen and politicians were permanent fixtures in Austin because the State Capitol was down the street from Texas Memorial Stadium. These men were accustomed to getting what they wanted. Winning football games was on their priority list. Over the next twenty years, Darrell would report to seven different University presidents. The average tenure of a UT President was three and a half years. Bible had already given Darrell the word— "Stay away from the Capitol," the old man whispered. Politics could destroy a university president or a football coach in an instant.

Texas politics are fraught with peril. For evidence, one only has to look at the fall of 2014. Over a matter of months, The University of Texas system Board of Regents managed to fire or force out Mack Brown, the head football coach, DeLoss Dodds, the Athletic Director, and Bill Powers, President of the University. An article in the *Texas Observer* dated July 8, 2014 highlighted the carnage surrounding Powers' departure. In Powers's case, he was fired on a Regents' vote of five to four.

In the spring of 1957, Darrell received a congratulatory telegram from A&M head coach Bear Bryant. It simply said, "Welcome Aboard," meaning welcome to the Southwest Conference. The SWC was founded in 1914 on a motion by The University of Texas. Some might say that UT made all the important moves over the next eighty two years of SWC play and that it patronized the other member institutions. The first organizational meeting was chaired by UT's L. Theo Bellmont at the Oriental Hotel in Dallas. Eight charter universities signed on, including The University of Oklahoma. (OU would leave the SWC after 1919.) Texas and OU had already established a fierce rivalry by that time, so the two institutions agreed to continue playing annually in Dallas as part of the Texas State Fair festivities.

There were extensive fluctuations in membership in the SWC in its early years. Rice University, for example, left the conference in 1916 only to rejoin in 1918. By the time Darrell Royal arrived in Austin, the Southwest Conference was settled as an organization of Texas institutions with the University of Arkansas as an additional member. The SWC began administering the annual Cotton Bowl Classic in 1940, and thus provided the SWC champion a direct path to bowl participation and to valuable prestige.

If it's true that "the past is prologue," as is carved in the granite monument in front of the National Archives in Washington, D.C., then people might conclude that the University of Texas and Texas A&M have been at war since birth. In the beginning, the war was about money. It was also about respect. Texas A&M was established in 1871 as a branch of the University of Texas. The legislature's original intent was that A&M would be a military school—with an all-male corps of cadets. The University of Texas opened in 1883 on forty acres within walking distance of the State Capitol. The geography gave UT a distinct advantage in lobbying the legislative and executive branches for scarce resources. The original battle between the military school and the elite school raged on. Finally, in order to stanch the bloodletting, UT was established with its own Board of

Regents while A&M continued with its separate Board of Directors. Skirmishes over money and foolish pride have continued for over a century because survival in Texas has always depended on garnering the most money and the most attention. By 1914, A&M's association with the Southwest Conference began and would continue until the Southwest Conference was dissolved in 1996, at which point both Texas and Texas A&M joined the Big Twelve.

Paul "Bear" Bryant played football at the University of Alabama while he was an undergraduate from 1933 to 1935. Like Jim Tatum, Bud Wilkinson, and numerous other college football coaches, he was influenced by his experiences coaching during World War II. Bryant coached at Georgia Pre-Flight and North Carolina Pre-Flight. Flight training took much longer than infantry and artillery training, so they built sports teams around the flyboys to boost morale. Bryant came to Texas A&M after serving as head coach at Maryland for one year in 1945, and at the University of Kentucky for eight years from 1946 to 1953. Coach Bryant discovered a young man named John David Crow in Springhill, Louisiana, near the Arkansas state line. Crow was quite large compared to running backs of his era. He stood six foot two and weighed 220 pounds. During Bryant's four-year coaching career at A&M, John David Crow would become the University's most celebrated player. In 1956, Crow was on the first Aggie team to defeat UT at their home stadium in Austin.

However, with the arrival of Darrell Royal in Austin in the spring of 1957, the tables turned on Bryant and Crow. The Longhorns shut down the vaunted Aggie rushing attack and prevailed at College Station's Kyle Field, nine to seven. Crow won the Heisman Trophy award after that season, an accomplishment that no one at A&M would repeat until Johnny Manziel's Heisman was awarded in 2013.

Coach Royal developed an appreciation for a Mississippi high school coach, Mike Campbell, who joined Darrell's UT staff. Campbell would eventually become Royal's defensive lieutenant. While Texas oligarchs looked on, Royal started winning football games. His teams defeated Texas A&M every year during Royal's first seven seasons at the helm of the Longhorns. He also defeated his mentor, Bud Wilkinson, and his Oklahoma alma mater six out of seven seasons. During the same period, his teams won four Southwest Conference titles in 1959, 1961, 1962, and 1963. Each of these led to Cotton Bowl matchups, of which the Longhorns won two and lost two.

The Texas faithful were pleased with the progress Coach Royal was making, despite not having earned a national championship. Away from the sidelines, Darrell was in demand as a speaker at civic clubs, high school banquets, and coaching clinics. Winning was giving him more confidence as a public speaker. Audiences were receptive to his personal charm and humorous, disarming country quips.

OU's Bud Wilkinson invented the television coach's show. The first such broadcast occurred on a Thursday evening—October 1, 1953—on WKY TV in Oklahoma City. Advertising executive Howard Newman was the studio host and Ned Hockman, an OU film and television professor in the OU journalism school, manned the main camera. In those days, studios existed only at television stations. Filming the *Bud Wilkinson Show* was problematic and the broadcast crew set up in a room in Oklahoma City's Municipal Auditorium. It was the same building where a youthful serviceman and his bride, Edith Royal, had gone to see live country and western music. In its early days, the *Bud Wilkinson Show* was only fifteen minutes long. However, Howard Newman and WKY negotiated a plum arrangement for the new show. Bud's show would come on at seven-thirty in the evening, right after *Groucho Marx* and before Jack Webb's popular series, *Dragnet*. The show was a hit in part because Bud had become an icon in the state and had built a football powerhouse. Additionally, Bud's smooth voice and poised articulation delighted his audience. Most college football coaches of the day lacked the polish to pull off being on stage. Darrell Royal, however, had the charisma. His burgeoning success in the late-1950s eventually led him to the television studio and his own show.

The Big Eight Conference was labeled "Oklahoma and the Seven Dwarfs," but by 1959, that moniker no longer applied. The Sooners under Wilkinson had a remarkable run that included a thirty-one game winning streak from 1948 through 1950 and a stunning streak of forty-seven games won from 1953 to 1957. The latter streak remains the current record for major college football wins. Wilkinson won three national championships—in 1950, 1955, and 1956. Some historians maintain that the 1956 Oklahoma Sooners were the greatest college football team of all time. That team won ten straight games and out of the ten opponents, six failed to score at all.

Bill Rives, sports editor of the *Dallas Morning News*, proclaimed that "the Oklahoma era is over" in his Sunday column following the 1959 OU-Texas game. Rives's observation proved prophetic. Texas won the 1959 contest nineteen to twelve after OU took an early twelve to nothing lead. Over the previous twelve years including 1959, Texas won only three times. The decade of the 1950s belonged to Oklahoma. As Darrell Royal would quip about the series, "This series is like grapes. Wins come in bunches." The Longhorns continued dominating OU in 1960 through 1962.

Sammy Mack Royal was born in Norman, Oklahoma in 1947 and subsequently accompanied the Royal family on the relocations they made over the decade, 1947-1957. Now, however, Mack was at home in Austin. He was old enough to rule Texas Memorial Stadium on Saturday afternoons. According to Mack, "I would go to the stadium early in the day and have lunch upstairs with the press, then I'd run around in the locker room and give the players trouble as they dressed, and then I'd go get a hot dog. The fans called me "Little Royal." Darrell was, for the most part, an absentee father. He was so driven as a coach that his children were left entirely to Edith's care. The family moved into a modest ranch style home west of campus on Belmont Parkway, a cul-de-sac back in the trees just off Lamar Avenue. The children could play safely there. Darrell failed to give the important parenting that children hunger for. There were about one-hundred kids over on the practice field; they were his first priority.

Reggie Grob grew up in Houston where he attended Spring Branch High School. He was a fine high school football player but was unlikely to realize his dream of playing for the University of

Texas. Reggie's desire and his tenacity were never in question. He stood five foot ten and weighed in at 200 pounds. Grob convinced his parents to let him walk onto the football team at UT, which he did in the fall of 1961. Grob did his best to survive his freshman season, 1961–1962. He relished in telling his classmates that he was on the football team and in cheering on his upper class teammates during their near-miss at a national championship that year. The 1961 Longhorns rolled through eight straight opponents and rose to the number one spot in the Associated Press rankings. But then a mediocre TCU team blindsided the Horns by a score of six to nothing. Texas finished out that season by hammering A&M and then defeating Ole Miss in the Cotton Bowl. Longhorn fans were understandably giddy about the team's chances for a national championship in the fall of 1962.

Coach Royal's stock was rising. Accolades poured in from the City of Austin and the state legislature proclaimed a Darrell Royal Day. These honors were bestowed in response to Darrell being named Coach of the Year by the Football Writers Association of America. The first ever Longhorn football banquet was held at Austin's Villa Capri Motel. Reggie was there with the team's stars of the day, George Sauer Junior, Pat Culpepper, Scott Appleton, Duke Carlisle, Ernie Koy Junior, Ray Poage, Tommy Ford, and Marvin Kristynik.

In retrospect, it was sufficient for Reggie Grob to be a minor part of something as grand as Texas football. The truest form of amateurism is reflected in young men like Grob. On September 1, 1962, the first day of UT's grueling two-a-day practices, a combination of commitment and excessive pride claimed Reggie Grob's life. Grob collapsed from heat exhaustion under the afternoon sun and was admitted to Brackenridge Hospital. Over the next seventeen days, Grob's condition worsened and was complicated by kidney failure, liver failure, and internal bleeding. Grob was flown from Austin to Dallas's Parkland Hospital for surgery to address the kidney failure, after which Reggie fell into a coma. After five days of worsening conditions, Reggie died. It was said later that Coach Royal authorized Grob to be the first walk-on at UT to also be awarded a scholarship. Perhaps. Or Coach Royal in saying so was only doing damage control. In any event, Royal was on the practice field when word of Reggie's death came. Edith Royal later said, "That was the closest [Darrell] ever came to quitting in all of those years of coaching. He felt he had failed to take care of one of his players."

The Spring Branch School District renamed its high school stadium Reggie Grob Stadium. In 2007, some forty-five years after Reggie's death, there was a photo opportunity at the high school stadium to highlight renovations. Reggie's father's attendance was requested, and he did attend, wheeled around in his wheelchair. In every frame shot by photographers that day, Mister Grob's facial expression is the same—lips drawn tight and sadness in his eyes reflecting a melancholy that never leaves.

By 1996, the University of Texas had experienced twenty post-Royal years which were unsatisfactory, at least by UT standards. Additionally, the Southwest Conference had been dissolved. UT was joining the Big Twelve Conference, which was a consolidation of the Big Eight and the four most powerful members of the SWC. The Longhorns needed a boost. UT President Robert Berdahl and Athletic Director DeLoss Dodds arranged a luncheon with Darrell at Barton Creek Country Club. Berdahl and Dodds told Coach Royal they wanted to change the name of Texas Memorial Stadium to the Darrell K Royal Texas Memorial Stadium. The gentlemen wanted Darrell's consent, which he happily offered. The idea of re-naming the stadium, Royal-Grob Texas Memorial Stadium never occurred to any of them.

A radiant Edith Thomason smiles outside her family home, circa 1944.

The Thomason homestead near the banks of the Salt Fork in Old Greer County, Oklahoma.

Cub Thomason checks the weather out the kitchen window before heading to the fields.

Grandfather Thomason and Grandson David Kazen on the Thomason place.

Cub Thomason shows off his corn crop. Cub was rarely without his bib overalls and hat.

Addie Mae Thomason gets her laundry hung out on the line to dry.

The Royal boys of Hollis, Oklahoma. Glenn, Don, Ray and the youngest, Darrell, circa 1942.

Darrell was good at every sport. Here he plays baseball for the Will Rogers Eagles while stationed at Will Rogers Field, Oklahoma City.

OU All-American Darrell Royal poses on Picture Day on the practice field, Norman, Oklahoma, 1949.

Young girls wait to get Darrell's autograph on Picture Day, circa 1949.

Darrell and his coach and mentor, Bud Wilkinson, remained close always.

Darrell and children Mack and Marian visit the OU Infirmary, circa 1951.

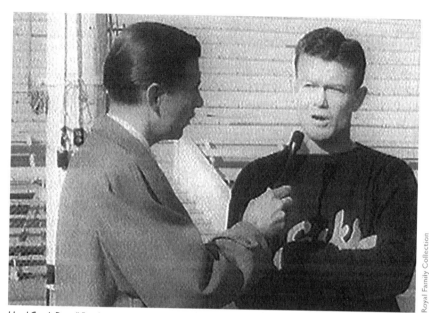

Head Coach Darrell Royal is interviewed on camera by a reporter covering the Edmonton Eskimos football team, 1953.

Darrell and David Wade at home in Starkville, Mississippi, where Darrell was head coach of the Mississippi State Bulldogs, 1954.

Coach Royal instructs his Longhorn players on the practice field, Austin, Texas, circa 1963.

Despite being self-conscious about his public speaking, Darrell's effort at improvement, along with his personal charm, carried the day on his weekly televised coaches show.

Marian enjoys a fall weekend in the backyard of her home in Austin on Belmont Parkway, wearing her Dad's vintage Oklahoma Sooner jersey.

A pensive David Wade Royal.

Mack Royal as a teenager, eventually suffered the stresses of the household that distanced him from his father.

Marian, her husband Chic Kazen, and children Christian and David pose for a photo on David's christening day.

Darrell Royal and Bud Wilkinson photographed on Owen Field, Norman, Oklahoma. Our heroes are never as perfect as we would like them to be.

Darrell and Edith loved being in the company of celebrities, as is evidenced by their friendship with the Sausage King, Jimmy Dean.

Darrell and Willie Nelson were running buddies for years. Pickin' parties at the Royal home were regular events..

Grateful benefactors gave Darrell a burnt orange Corvette Stingray. David Wade and a friend took the car on a joy ride to Hollis, Oklahoma, before the car was given to Darrell's friend and assistant coach, Mike Campbell.

Traveling in style. Access to private jets was a part of the Royal's ongoing friendships with the Texas rich and famous.

Casa Thompson, Cuernavaca, Mexico. John Philip Thompson, then CEO of 7-Eleven/Southland Corporation headquartered in Dallas, gave his estate to the Royals for their use one month every summer.

Former President Lyndon Johnson and Lady Bird hosted Darrell and Edith for a group vacation in Acapulco, Mexico, after LBJ's retirement from office. Johnson had use of an estate owned by a former President of Mexico.

From left, Darrell Royal, Lee Jamail, Joe Jamail, and an unidentified lady. Darrell and Joe were close friends for many years.

Verdict day in the Pennzoil vs. Texaco civil litigation. Joe Jamail and Darrell Royal celebrate the 12.1 billion dollar judgment in favor of Jamail's client, Pennzoil.

Darrell and Edith's new home under construction in Jim Bob Moffett's Barton Creek Development in west Austin.

From left, Mack Royal, Christian Kazen, Edith Royal, Darrell Royal, David Kazen, Elena Trombetta, and unidentified young man, at the Royal home for the holidays.

The old warriors, Darrell Royal and Frank Broyles, are honored at a football game in Austin.

From their youthful days in Hollis, Oklahoma, they were a marvelous team. It was always Darrell and Edith.

REVOLUTION

T he life of a college football coach and to a large extent, the lives of the athletes he coaches, exist in a vacuum. The pressure cooker of big time athletic competition demands a focus and discipline every day of the year. There is irony in these circumstances, given that college is intended to expose young people to new ideas and challenges. That is, after all, how young people grow. Cultural shifts are bound to creep into the lives and values of college students and athletes in particular. While college athletic participation is a rigid conservative undertaking similar to military service, those requirements can be tested by a tumultuous sometimes defiant, youth culture.

Jack Kerouac, the father of the Beat Generation, died in 1969 at the age of forty-seven. In life, he was a literary iconoclast who pioneered a new method of writing along with fellow Beats Allen Ginsburg and William S. Burroughs. As a young man, Kerouac was an athlete sufficiently gifted to earn football scholarships by Notre Dame, Boston College, and Columbia. Kerouac made his way to Columbia where his football career was cut short by injuries. More significantly, Kerouac was constantly challenging the authority of the coaching staff. Head coach Lou Little did what coaches do to rein in belligerents—he benched Jack. Instead, Jack quit the team and dropped out of Columbia. In the Greenwich Village community in lower Manhattan, Kerouac encountered like-minded free thinkers such as Ginsburg, Burroughs, and Neal Cassaday. Kerouac's notebook scribblings became, without editing, "spontaneous prose." When asked later about his work, he said he wrote about man's simple revolt from society as it is, with all its inequalities, frustrations, and self-inflicted agonies. For years, New York publishers rejected Kerouac's book, *On the Road*, finding it to be too sympathetic toward minorities and other marginalized social groups of post-World War II America. The manuscript was also deemed too graphic in its descriptions of drug use and homosexuality. These same reservations were later expressed about William S. Burroughs's *Naked Lunch* and Ginsburg's masterpiece, *Howl*.

By 1957, a heavily-edited version of *On the Road* was accepted for publication. Upon its release, the *New York Times* book review called Kerouac "the voice of a new generation." Children of World War II veterans embraced the clarion call to question authority. At the same time, Kerouac's newfound celebrity made him uncomfortable. He was being dragged into mainstream society against his will by book editors who wanted to purchase his future work. Kerouac viewed these entreaties as people trying to "purchase his soul." As a result, he was always on the move. Other members of the Beat Generation had taken up residence in San Francisco's North Beach in order to live communally near Lawrence Ferlinghetti's bookstore, City Lights. Freedom of thought—freedom of behavior—was celebrated in disjointed prose and poetry readings at City Lights. A nearby run-down neighborhood known as Haight-Ashbury began filling up with migrating young people. Seekers of all nature and description shared their thoughts, their bodies, and their creativity willingly and without expectation. The counterculture was likewise taking root in Greenwich Village in New York. The seeds of the movement were taking root in Austin, Texas, as well. When Kerouac died, he became a symbol of an entire generation eager to effect change. Kerouac's simple grave marker carries only the inscription, "He Honored Life."

The emerging counterculture was colliding head-on with the traditional values of post-war American society. After all, American democracy had triumphed over Nazi tyranny. Americans felt validated by their sacrifice and resulting victory. Young veterans started families, thus creating the "Baby Boom." These members of what would become known as "The Greatest Generation" embraced the promises of prosperity full tilt. Some went to college on the GI Bill; others started small businesses. Almost all attended church regularly. The Supreme Allied Commander, General Dwight Eisenhower, entered the White House in 1952 along with a California politician as Vice President, Richard Nixon. Conformity to social norms was so pronounced that in 1955, author Sloan Wilson penned *The Man in the Gray Flannel Suit* to address what he observed as a growing danger. Two-time presidential nominee Adlai Stevenson, a professorial sort, described America as being subsumed in crisis defined as "collectivism colliding with individualism." The public ignored much of this debate as citizens continued to climb up the economic ladder within corporations and smaller enterprises. This prevailing philosophy applied to every aspect of life including the paramilitary pastime of sporting Americans—college football. Darrell Royal's intensity, discipline and commitment were reflective of the times.

The United States had military advisors stationed in French Indochina as early as 1950 during the Truman administration. After the Japanese surrender in 1945 and the failures of Churchill, Roosevelt, and Stalin to resolve outstanding territorial issues, more war was inevitable. General Douglas MacArthur became military governor of Japan after WWII and completely ignored the Soviet Union's involvement in the matter. MacArthur set about to introduce democracy into a carefully crafted new civil society. Emperor Hirohito's life was spared. In fact, he was allowed to retain his title as emperor but only for ceremonial contexts. A new Japanese constitution was drafted. A democratic Parliament was established.

Land reform placed farmlands under individual ownership. Labor unions grew. Policymakers in the Soviet Union and China viewed all of these developments with growing alarm. China's huge expanse shared boundaries with the Korean Peninsula on the north and Indochina on the south. Additional aggravation could be traced to the historical conflict between the Japanese and Chinese people. In this unstable climate, the Soviet Union declared war on Japan in August, 1945 and by agreement with the United States, occupied Korea north of the thirty-eighth parallel. The Japanese subsequently surrendered to the Soviets, which led to settled claims in the north while the focus shifted south. Despite an interim agreement regarding division of territory, North Korea invaded South Korea in June of 1950, thus initiating the latest proxy war between the Soviet Union and the United States. For three years, American soldiers were embroiled in an Asian war which ended not with formal resolution but with an armistice in July of 1953. With the benefit of hindsight, it is easy to see how mistrust between the United States, the Soviet Union, and China helped the conflicts to unfold. The predictable result was the Soviet war against Japan followed by the Korean War followed by the Vietnam War.

Many historians believe that had President Kennedy lived to see a 1964 re-election, he would have withdrawn American forces from Vietnam. Instead, President Johnson continually committed additional forces to Vietnam. He adhered to the "domino theory," the belief that failure to halt communism's expansion in Vietnam would lead to other southeast Asians countries falling to communist control like dominoes.

Against this historical backdrop, the late 1960s featured the trauma of televised reports from Vietnam. Body bags were arriving at a Delaware military base daily. The average American could not understand the mission in a tiny Asian country so far away. Some observers began to doubt whether the nation's military could be trusted to report truthfully the news from the front. In 1964, a purported attack on a U.S. reconnaissance vessel in the Gulf of Tonkin spawned American outrage. That outrage led to what became known as the Gulf of Tonkin Resolution in Congress, which gave President Johnson full rein to authorize a war against the North Vietnamese aggressors. Years later, the purported military engagement in the Gulf of Tonkin proved to be false. General William Westmoreland embodied mistrust for the doves in Congress and also became the object of contempt by Vietnam protestors in the streets across the country, including in the streets of Austin. As the number of casualties grew, so did the country's polarization about the Vietnam War. The same countercultural communities that emerged a few years earlier were transformed into armies of young people practicing protest and civil disobedience. In Austin, bohemians found additional common ground by challenging authority on all levels and in all venues.

Guadalupe Street, also known as "the Drag," runs along the west edge of the UT campus in Austin. By 1965, the drag was teeming with barefoot young people, some of whom were students, some not. They played music on guitars, flutes, and tambourines. They hawked homemade jewelry, beads, and tie-dyed t-shirts. The entire scene evoked a communal spirit and the central themes were peace and love. The related values were anti-war and anti-authority.

Marian Royal, who was still in high school at Stephen F. Austin High School, was drawn to the Drag and all its energy. Her interest in art lured her toward its aura of creativity. Her time there led her to radical political ideas. Social issues such as race relations, war, and drug use occupied her thoughts. She read Kerouac's *On the Road* as every young bohemian had. She read *Black like Me*, the 1961 novel which set her on a path to seeking social justice. By the time she had turned eighteen and enrolled at UT, she was spending much of her spare time in east Austin among the young black community there. Edith Royal was concerned about this behavior. Marian's hippie clothing, her suspected drug experimentation, and her black friends led Edith and Darrell to worry that their daughter's activities would be discovered by the UT administration and, worst of all, by the local media. Marian's social activism and rebelliousness ran counter to the discipline Darrell demanded of his players on the football field.

Austin was home to an active, industrious Lebanese community of merchants, lawyers, and judges. Clifford Antone was one such businessman. His music venue, Antone's, attracted large audiences every night of the week. Promising musicians could get a career break by appearing on the stage at Antone's. Through Clifford Antone and his Lebanese connections, Marian met a young, ambitious UT law student, Abraham "Chic" Kazen III, from Laredo, Texas. Chic's father, Abraham Kazen, Junior—also known as "Chic"—was a powerful political figure in west Texas. The elder Kazen was a lawyer, a World War II combat veteran, and a Texas state legislator. The elder Kazen harbored grand ambitions for his namesake. Perhaps for this reason, Chic Kazen III began dating Marian Royal. Noted Houston attorney Joe Jamail, himself of Lebanese descent, attested to the Royals that the Lebanese Kazen clan of Laredo was upstanding. The budding romance was therefore encouraged by both families. Edith was particularly enthusiastic. Even though Marian was only nineteen years old, she married Chic Kazen III on Sunday, December 27, 1964 at the Kazen family's church, Saint Austin's Catholic. Afterwards, the newlyweds continued their studies at UT. Marian earned her BFA degree in 1967 and Chic earned his law degree in 1968. All of this was accomplished just as Chic Kazen, Junior was taking office as a U.S. Congressman from the Texas Twenty-Third District. Chic III and Marian moved to Washington, D.C. in order to be groomed for their ascent up the political and social ladders. Meanwhile, Marian gave birth to two sons, Christian and David, in that order. However, the suffocating Washington scene rattled Marian. It was so far removed from her friends in Austin that she was bewildered in many ways. Unlike her father-in-law and husband, she hadn't developed a case of Potomac Fever.

In Austin, Darrell remained focused on building a football program the likes of which Texas had never experienced. The Texas elites were impressed with Coach Royal's successes since his arrival in Austin in 1957. Since that time, Royal had beaten Texas A&M six straight times and Oklahoma five straight times, and had appeared in five bowl games and won two of them. Prior to Royal's arrival, Texas hadn't been to a bowl game since 1952.

The tipping point for the Texas Longhorns seemed imminent. The 1962 team had spent time ranked number one in the UPI poll before tying Rice. Texas entered the 1963 battle with Oklahoma undefeated. Two weeks earlier, the Sooners had stunned the defending national champions, the USC Trojans, seventeen to twelve. USC was ranked number one at the time. That game was spectacular in many ways as it was played in the Los Angeles Coliseum on national television in 110-degree heat.

One fall day in October, 1963, Darrell's stars were aligned. OU came into the Red River Shootout ranked number one in the country by the Associated Press. The Texas Longhorns had rolled through its three prior opponents, Tulane, Texas Tech, and Oklahoma State without breaking a sweat. However, on this day, abundant sweat and blood were sacrificed. Texas dominated from the start. Oklahoma was flat, which vexed OU Coach Wilkinson. The final score was Texas twenty-eight, Oklahoma seven. Darrell led the Longhorns through the regular season undefeated and won Texas's first national championship. Despite the well-earned glory of the moment, Darrell's life was about to become more complicated.

Forty days and forty nights later, on November 22, 1963, President John F. Kennedy paid a political visit to Dallas to campaign and to patch up a political feud between Texas Governor John Connally and United States Senator Ralph Yarborough. According to authors Bill Minutaglio and Steven L. Davis in *Dallas 1963*, there was far more private discord in the Dallas community than the public discord between Connally and Yarborough. The picture these authors paint in describing Dallas is of a city crammed with larger than life characters of radical ultra-conservative political persuasion who called the shots in Dallas, as evidenced by their organization of an ad hoc policy-making group, the Dallas Citizens Council. The authors note, "The wood-lined, top floors of the downtown buildings, where the city's future is daily mapped out by men from the Dallas Citizens Council—and where the million-dollar oil and real estate contracts are signed, where the fate of the entire Dallas school system is being shaped, where the very look of entire neighborhoods is really decided." "It begins in the hushed dining rooms at the Republic Bank, inside the private club atop the Baker Hotel, in the <u>Dallas Morning News</u> executive offices, even in the pastor's office at First Baptist. Dallas is still tight that way, coordinated that way." Whatever President Kennedy knew about this unseemly situation did not deter him from climbing into an open Lincoln limousine and heading west along Elm Street toward Dealey Plaza and past the Texas School Book Depository.

For many Dallasites on that day, the last time they stood on the sidewalks of downtown Dallas was during the State Fair Parade they witnessed the previous October 12 just prior to the Oklahoma-Texas game in the Cotton Bowl Stadium. Now it was time to see Texas political royalty and the President of the United States up close and personal. Earlier in the day, President Kennedy settled a squabble between Connally and Yarborough over who would ride with whom in the motorcade. Yarborough represented the liberal wing of the Texas Democratic Party and wanted nothing to do with Governor Connally. JFK pulled Senator Yarborough aside and whispered, "If you value our friendship, you will do this." And so it was that the reconciliation involved Connally and his wife Nellie riding in the President's car in the jumpseats just in front of JFK and Jackie while Yarborough rode with Vice President Johnson in a limousine with Lady Bird Johnson sitting in the middle between them. After the violent horrors of that afternoon, Lyndon Baines Johnson of Texas was sworn in as the thirty-sixth President of the United States on Air Force One by federal judge Sarah Hughes, a friend of Johnson's. Larger than life characters in Dallas and beyond were now positioned to impose their will on every aspect of life in Texas and across the country.

The Longhorns completed their season undefeated and went to the Cotton Bowl game where they defeated Navy, led by Heisman Trophy winner Roger Staubach, twenty-eight to six. Texas was the only college team who did not lose a game in 1963. Both the Associated

Press and United Press International named the Longhorns national champions. Darrell took the congratulatory call from President Johnson in that steamy postgame Cotton Bowl locker room. Darrell told a friend shortly thereafter, "We'd accomplished what we came to Texas to do—everything we'd set our minds to do."

Lyndon Johnson didn't go to college at the University of Texas. Rather, he attended Southwest Texas State University in San Marcos, intent upon becoming a school teacher. His life took a turn when he became a field aide to Congressman Richard Kleberg of Texas's Tenth Congressional District after a short stint teaching in a rural Hispanic community. The Kleberg family owned the famous mega-ranch that is known today as the King Ranch. In his position as aide, Johnson was exposed to wealth and power for the first time. He was attracted to both. Claudia Alta Taylor's background was materially different from Lyndon's. Lady Bird might have been born in East Texas, but she was raised according to Alabama's rituals of gentility. She had her first personal account at Neiman Marcus when she was sixteen. She traveled in the United States and Europe extensively with her girlfriends. In short, she was a young woman with a wealthy southern pedigree, two degrees from the University of Texas, and access to her inheritance. Lyndon was no doubt aware of these facts. He proposed marriage on their first date, which included breakfast at Austin's Driskill Hotel followed by a drive though Texas hill country. Lady Bird was both stunned and flattered. A mere ten weeks later, she accepted Lyndon's proposal. They were married in November of 1934.

A seasoned politician was once asked about the secret of his political success. "Why," he answered, "you see a vacuum and you move into it." These words are applicable to many of life's successes, including those in power politics and coaching college football. According to noted LBJ biographer, Robert Caro, LBJ always felt a bit inadequate because unlike Lady Bird and the political mentors around him in Austin, he hadn't attended the state's flagship university. And, as in all things LBJ took an interest in over the next fifty years, he set about to compensate for any perceived shortcoming. The visual evidence is the huge edifice of the LBJ Library which sits just northeast of the football stadium on the UT-Austin campus today.

Since political winners migrate to other winners, it's no surprise that LBJ was the most notable among the many powerful Texans that migrated to Darrell K Royal. "My phone would ring at home in the evening and a lady would say, 'Coach Royal, please hold for the President.'" Johnson didn't give two hoots about football, but he cared about whatever it was that powerful Texans cared about, so he cared about the coach of the Texas Longhorns—the reigning national champions. "The President would ask me, 'Darrell, why don't you call me once in a while?' I'd say, Mister President, I know you're very busy and I hate to bother you. 'Now Darrell,' LBJ would say, 'you call me just like you'd call your mama.'" Darrell remained focused on football and didn't quite grasp that his newfound rich and powerful friends included many who would move into the political vacuum created by the events of the fall of 1963. Darrell was unaware that the Dallas Citizens Council was not the only shadowy organization in the state of Texas and that such informal groups expected to control every important policy matter in the state.

Darrell was a hard-nosed, competitive football taskmaster but had a softer side with the general public. This served him well throughout his career. He and Edith loved people. They grew up that way back in Hollis, Oklahoma. Both also had enormous energy complemented by tolerance that they carried with them everywhere. They found themselves invited to all the significant social and political gatherings of the day. They would be prominently seated next to corporate titans, elected officials, and others of high ambition. Dallas, Houston, and San Antonio became frequent stops along with Tyler, Amarillo, and El Paso. They took it all in and loved every minute of it, basking in burnt orange glory.

Donnie Fox recalled, "As Darrell used to say when we were riding around together on the dusty streets of Hollis, The sun don't shine on the same ole dog's ass every day." But in the fall of 1963 and into 1964, the sun was shining on Darrell K Royal. A few weeks later, a wealthy oil man from Houston called Darrell at home. The oil man invited Darrell to drive down to Houston and meet with a group of fellows that the oil man said he needed to know. Like the shadowy activities of the self-appointed Dallas Citizens Council—like the Big Tex mannequin at State Fair Park—things are larger than life in Texas. And not always what they seem.

WHITE

The euphoria that enveloped the State of Texas following UT's first national championship win elevated Darrell K Royal to heroic status. The accompanying limelight thrilled Darrell and Edith. They derived great satisfaction from traveling across the state and nation to be recognized at banquets and coaching clinics. Gifts from grateful benefactors poured into the coach's stadium office. Newspaper writers speculated that Royal would make a fine governor.

The seminal year of 1963 produced a wave of change in Austin prior to the final victory of the season over Roger Staubach and the Navy Midshipmen in the Cotton Bowl. Momentous political and cultural benchmarks were opened to examination and opinion. Texas' unique history had begun, in fact, with the decisive victory over Santa Anna's Mexican army in 1836. That victory and the Mexican-American War in general spawned a permanent sense of exceptionality among Texans. Only the state of Texas could boast a history of being an independent republic. That status began in 1836 and ended with statehood a decade later, in 1845. However, in February of 1861, Texas seceded from the Union and promptly joined the Confederate States of America. The legislature's declaration of causes attached to the Act of Secession accused northern politicians and abolitionists of committing a series of outrages upon Texas. Prominent among the causes was Texas's defense of slavery and white supremacy. Other than South Carolina, the Texas legislature voted the highest percentage of support for secession among the cotton states. The subsequent statewide referendum was likewise lopsided, and secession was approved by a vote of 46,129 to 14,697. After the Civil War, Texas became a haven for southerners fleeing the physical and emotional devastation brought on by fighting for the "Lost Cause."

The grandsons of these scarred but proud southerners became the titans of Texas oil, industry, politics, and commerce a scant fifty years after General Lee's surrender at Appomattox. One hundred years after the South surrendered, while the wounds of battle were bound up, the principles set forth in the declaration of secession remained the core social values in corporate board rooms and gentile, all-white country clubs. Today, a Confederate monument still sits on the south lawn of the State Capitol in Austin.

In today's Texas, the remnants of Civil War humiliation coupled with an equal measure of support for states' rights surfaces from time to time. Modern secessionists exist in Texas. Their efforts picked up steam in the 1990s and eventually morphed into the Texas Nationalist Movement. Ultra-conservative politicians seeking to curry favor with the secessionists have granted some sense of legitimacy to the movement. Former Governor Rick Perry stumbled through comments that can be interpreted as a veiled threat to pursue Texas secession. President Obama's re-election in 2012 prompted the printing of bumper stickers and yard signs declaring "Secede!" A proud history that began with the establishment of the Republic of Texas continues to ripple across the political landscape of the State.

Native Texan Bryan Burrough's 2009 book, *The Big Rich: The Rise and Fall of the Greatest Texas Oil Fortunes* states, "If you want to understand the Texas soul, it's a complicated thing; a roiling psychic stew of narcissism, ambition, brilliance, humor, vengefulness, pettiness, fearlessness, and of course, a bottomless pit of need." One of Burrough's subjects, Roy Cullen of Houston, "dreamed of restoring his mother's massive white plantation home someday, with its porticos and rose trellises and gardens, just like the beloved family plantation the hated Union men had burned." Two other Burroughs subjects, Sid Richardson and Clint Murchison, Senior, used their wealth and ultra-conservative political views in different ways. The men grew up as boyhood friends in Athens, Texas. Today there is a private members-only rod and gun club just south of Athens with historical ties to the two oil titans. Its name is the Koon Kreek Club.

Across the Red River to the north, Oklahoma's history was decidedly different. It was Indian Territory during the Civil War and did not attain statehood until 1907. Prejudices existed in to be sure. But integration came along earlier nonetheless.

Prentice Gautt was a fine high school athlete in Oklahoma City at Douglass High School who graduated in the spring of 1956. Oklahoma had won its second national championship the preceding fall. Thus it was no surprise that Gautt dreamed of playing for the Sooners. There was one issue, however. Gautt was black. Coach Wilkinson and a group of prominent black civic leaders from Oklahoma City did what they could to smooth the way for Prentice's enrollment at OU and his active participation in football. Gautt became an outstanding student and a fine football player at OU and earned All-Big Eight honors in both 1958 and 1959. For many years, Gautt served as associate commissioner of the Big Eight Conference, representing in a very personal way all that is wholesome and honorable about college football.

Frank Broyles, head coach at the University of Missouri in 1957, signed Mizzou's first black scholarship football players, Norris Swenson and Mel West. At that time, Jim Crow laws were pervasive in Columbia restaurants, motels, and public facilities, as they were throughout Missouri. Broyles requested and received permission from his athletic director, Don Faurot, to begin recruiting black athletes. It was all in keeping with the Missouri Plan, devised by Faurot to recruit only Missouri natives to the campus. By 1958, however, Broyles had moved on to the University of Arkansas in the Southwest Conference, joining the University of Texas and other Texas institutions. According to Broyles, the Arkansas Board of Regents made it clear he was not to recruit black athletes to Arkansas.

1963 was a tumultuous year. Martin Luther King, Junior stood on the steps of the Lincoln Memorial and delivered his "I have a dream" speech during the March on Washington. FBI Director J. Edgar Hoover, a personal friend and business associate of Texas oil tycoon Sid Richardson, called King a radical with communist leanings and thus made King the object of government surveillance for the rest of his life. By October, 1964, King received the Nobel Peace Prize for combating racial inequality through nonviolence. In 1965, King helped organize the people's march from Selma, Alabama to Montgomery, which had been preceded by "Bloody Sunday" on the Edmund Pettus Bridge in Selma.

George Corley Wallace was sworn in as Governor of Alabama on January 14, 1963, standing on the exact spot where Jefferson Davis was sworn in as provisional president of the Confederate States of America 102 years earlier. In his inaugural address, Wallace declared his infamous line: "In the name of the greatest people that have trod on this earth, I draw the line in the dust and toss down the gauntlet before the feet of tyranny and say segregation now, segregation tomorrow, and segregation forever!"

Since 1961, black students at the University of Texas had peacefully protested segregation on the UT campus by picketing Board of Regents meetings to call for integration and social justice. In July of 1961, the UT Regents reacted by defiantly passing a resolution that confirmed segregation of campus dormitories with the rationale that housing was "auxiliary to the educational process." Richard Pennington's 1987 book, *Breaking the Ice: The Racial Integration of Southwest Conference Football*, chronicles the glacial movement in integrating athletics in the Southwest Conference and at the University of Texas in particular. There were, ironically, powerful forces working to desegregate all aspects of university life on the UT campus.

Governor John Connally appointed Dallas lawyer Frank Erwin to the UT Board of Regents. Significantly, Lyndon Johnson had two daughters attending UT at the time. As Vice President, he worried that media attention would embarrass him and possibly impede his lofty political ambitions. According to author Pennington, LBJ engaged in some friendly arm-twisting with Regents Board Chairman W. W. Heath, imploring him to desegregate or risk losing federal grants for the University. The Regents thereafter moved to alter university policies. By the fall of 1963, UT's most aggressive mover and shaker, Frank Erwin, had engineered a new policy making black athletes eligible for sports participation. Across campus, Coach Royal was caught in a bind. Official university policy was one thing. Implementation, while defying of the wishes of his major donors and personal benefactors was another. Pennington quotes Royal as saying about those years, "I wasn't exactly commanded or given an order but I was let known that we weren't to recruit black athletes. I didn't call the shots at the University of Texas." It would be 1970 before the University of Texas recruited and admitted black athletes into its football program.

The matter of race was appearing in unlikely places during the 1960s. In February of 1964, a young black boxer who won a gold medal in boxing at the 1962 Rome Olympics, Cassius Clay, stunned the sporting world by knocking out then-current world heavyweight champion, Sonny Liston. Clay represented a radical departure from the stereotypical boxers of the era. He was handsome, lean, confident, and charismatic. In a single night, black Americans gained a universal hero.

Coach Royal, as always, stayed focused on his coaching responsibilities and on accommodating the rich and powerful. All of this was part of his job description. His 1964 Longhorns came within a single point of another undefeated season. They had been stunned by Arkansas fourteen to thirteen in Austin. The Horns finished out the season by defeating Bear Bryant's Crimson Tide twenty-one to seventeen in the Cotton Bowl.

The first manifestations of turmoil on the Royal homefront

erupted in the summer of 1965. By then, daughter Marian had married the son of a United States Congressman and was living in Austin. The youngest Royal child, David Wade, was a rambunctious twelve-year old who was born in 1953. It was painfully clear to Mack, a high school senior-to-be, that David had won his father's heart. According to Mack, "Darrell was over the moon for David." Perhaps there was an explanation. Mack had no interest in athletics. He preferred the solitude of his room, building model airplanes, taking photographs of still life, or reading. He was, in short, an introspective, sensitive, vulnerable kid. David, on the other hand, was a genuine daredevil. He received his middle name from Darrell's close friend and OU teammate, Wade Walker. One can only speculate that Darrell saw a lot of himself in the reckless, carefree antics of his younger son. Mack certainly felt the pain of isolation. When Edith was asked years later why she thought Mack had become disillusioned and distant, she replied, "I just thought it must be that middle child curse, you know."

A neighbor of the Royals inherited a 1950 Ford with only 8,000 miles on it. Darrell paid 400 bucks for the automobile and it became Mack's mode of transportation. Predictably, Mack found his way to the Drag just as his sister had before him. The bohemians on the Drag had two essential commonalities—disillusionment with the status quo and distrust of authority. The same could certainly be said of Mack Royal. Because Mack had spending money, he was a prime candidate for experimentation and adventure. Disillusionment continued to fester. In one act of defiance, he announced to Darrell and Edith that he wanted to go to Hollis, Oklahoma for his senior year in high school. He felt that he could escape the discomfort of his home life by undertaking the grand adventure of living with his cousin, Tommy Darrell Royal. Coach Royal issued a terse response. "That ain't happenin', son." Mack continued to conjure up ways to escape Austin. After completing his senior year at Austin High, he again declared independence by telling his parents he wanted to go to California and explore the creative arts and his interest in photography. "No, you're not drivin' out to California. That car belongs to me and you're not taking it to California," said Darrell. The fact is that Darrell and Edith were concerned about Mack. They suspected much and knew some of his reckless habits. Mack announced he was going to California anyway. He hitchhiked all the way to Los Angeles. Upon returning to Austin some weeks later, he shared with his parents his wishes to go away to college. "No, you're going to UT. I've already arranged it. And you're going to live in Moore-Hill dormitory with the athletes." Mack was in despair. He followed his father's orders and moved into the jock dorm. He was involuntarily pre-enrolled as well. Mack was suffocating emotionally. Shoes became an option rather than a necessity. He only went to class on a whim. Viewing all of this first hand, Darrell and Edith determined Mack was in trouble. They arranged for Mack to receive treatment out of state. When he completed his program, he returned to Austin to live with others in a group home. "It was a good thing for Mack to live in the recovery home for a while," said Edith. "It may have saved his life." What treatment didn't do was stop Mack from resenting that his activities were controlled as thoroughly as if he was one of his dad's football players.

Quite by accident, Mack found an educational setting that appealed to him. Darrell was scheduled to be honored by Mississippi State University in Starkville. Mack accompanied him on the trip to Starkville to revisit where he'd spent a portion of his youth. While Darrell attended the festive campus events, Mack took a solo road trip through the countryside and wound up in Columbus, Mississippi. What Mack discovered was a beautiful little school, Mississippi College for Women. Despite its name, the college had become co-educational. Darrell and Edith, exasperated, agreed attending Mississippi College might be good for Mack. He studied computer science, found a girlfriend, and enjoyed the slower pace of Columbus. He was, finally, at peace with himself.

Other evidences of discord surfaced in Coach Royal's life.

"I never should have gone to the University of Texas. In fact, I never should have been recruited to play football at UT," said Glen Booher years after the fact. Glen was a senior at Oklahoma City's Northwest Classen High School in the spring of 1966. He recalled,

"We had a really good running back on our team, Johnny Johnson. Johnny was a good friend of mine and we both expected to play college ball somewhere. I wasn't in Johnny's league as a ball player, but I was highly motivated to go play and get my education paid for. Darrell Royal wanted Johnny Johnson badly. In those days there was a fifty-scholarship limit, in the Southwest Conference, double what it is today. Thus Texas offered "throwaway scholarships". A kid might receive a throwaway scholarship if attracting him would help land a much better teammate. These throwaway scholarships were also extended for political reasons. If an important booster wanted his kid to get an offer, the no-talent kid was extended a throwaway. I fell into the former category, not good enough to play at Texas but close enough to Johnny to encourage him to join me in Austin. You gotta remember, in the spring of 1966, OU was searching for a new head coach. There were several weeks when OU had no coaches at all out on the road recruiting. It was during this period that Johnny and I took our recruiting trip from Oklahoma City to Austin along with several recruits from Dallas Bryan Adams High School. Assistant Coach Bill Ellington was showing us around the UT campus when he took us to the library. At that moment, two black students were coming out the door, to whom Ellington said hello. After they had passed out of earshot, Coach Ellington leaned into our group and said, 'I'm sorry you guys had to see that. There sure aren't any blacks on our football team, I can tell you that.' In the end, Johnny Johnson went to OU and I took the offer to attend UT. I had a four-year scholarship to a fine university in hand and an opportunity to play for the Longhorns. Isn't that what college athletics is supposed to be about? Moore-Hill dormitory was the jock dorm. It had four or five floors with no elevators. Right away I noticed that all the blue-chippers were assigned rooms on the first or second floor. The higher up in the dorm you lived, the more insignificant you were to the program. I, of course, was assigned a room on the top floor. I'm sure that whenever the coaches looked at me, they remembered how they missed out on Johnny Johnson who had gone to their archrival. I went through all the so-called shit drills which were conducted after the top units had gone in from practice. Later on, I went through the Medina drills, conducted by UT trainer, Frank Medina. Those drills happened in a windowless, concrete block room underneath the stadium seats. It must have been 120 degrees in that room. We were ordered down on the floor in wrestling position. Medina said he was going to find out who was tough and who wasn't. There was no useful purpose in any of this other than to weed out the weak. By the second semester, the brain coach, Lan Hewlett, enrolled me in classes way over my head. I couldn't participate in class discussions at all. It took me a while to get my classes straightened out."

During spring practice in 1967, Booher tore up a knee. "My surgery was performed right there on campus at the student health center by Doctor John C. Buckley. I was hobbling around on crutches, going up and down those flights of stairs in Moore-Hill every day. I got a phone call from Coach Royal's secretary, Ruth Gold. She told me to come over that afternoon to the coach's office to sign some papers. She said they were just some insurance papers related to my knee surgery. I can remember hobbling over there in the heat, then up more stairs to Coach Royal's office. Mrs. Gold sat me down at her desk. Coach Royal was nowhere to be found. She handed me a sheaf of typewritten pages and pointed out where I was supposed to sign. As I scanned the pages, one in particular caught my eye. By signing, I was waiving my scholarship! I pushed my chair back so hard that it struck Mrs. Gold's office door. I told her I was not going to sign my scholarship away. No way. And I got up and hobbled out the door. Later on, I had to admit to myself that the heart necessary for playing football had been torn right out of me. I called my dad. He called Coach Royal and they had a very pointed discussion. I knew I wasn't going to play but I wasn't going to let them run me off either. I was going to get my degree."

There were other harsh realities that Booher observed during his years at UT. "We had Robby Layne out there on football scholarship. He was only out there because his dad was the great Bobby Layne. Robby came out as a placekicker but he wasn't worth a damn. In our spring game, Robby was sent out to attempt a field goal. He was so nervous, his kick struck the center right in the butt. When Happy Feller showed up, that was the end of Robby Layne." In the days to come, Booher played the cards he was dealt. In 1970, Booher received his degree from the University of Texas. He never earned a letter in football.

Royal Family Collection

GODS AND MORTALS

Bill Yeoman played football and basketball at Texas A&M
before embarking on a career coaching college football.
In December of 1961, he accepted the job as head football
coach at the University of Houston mostly to escape the
bone-chilling winters in East Lansing, Michigan where he had been
assistant coach. U of H was an obscure institution with mediocre
academics that catered to commuter students. It was also independent in collegiate sports. In the early 1960s, the campus was merely
a spread of squat buildings just west of the Gulf Freeway, south of
downtown. Anyone noticing U of H at all was likely heading somewhere further south such as the Houston Space Center or Galveston.
Lack of money, facilities, or a fan base left Coach Yeoman with scant
tools with which to build a program. His circumstances, did, however, change for the better. In July of 1963, construction began on
the Houston Astrodome—a wondrous indoor stadium. Judge Roy
Hofheinz was the Dome's patron saint. He was a former mayor of
Houston, a judge, and also a municipal administrator. A visionary
for his beloved city, he sought permanent tenants for the new domed

stadium to pay the bills. Rice University, the prestigious local university, was a member of the Southwest Conference but already had its own cavernous outdoor stadium on campus. The University of Houston Cougars, on the other hand, were a willing and available prospect. Coach Yeoman knew he could recruit athletes by promising they would play in the Astrodome. That same year, U of H integrated its athletic programs. In July of 1964, the most sought after running back in the State of Texas signed a letter of intent to attend Houston. Warren McVea's decision shocked the sporting world. He had been heavily recruited by the nation's best football institutions, but because McVea, an African American, had neither quality grades nor a sterling reputation for citizenship, he was considered a risk. Coach Yeoman, however, needed McVea desperately.

Yeoman brought with him from Michigan State an assistant, Chuck Fairbanks. Within a single school year, 1963–1964, the University of Houston Cougars had emerged from obscurity into a competitive, independent, notable athletic program. Promising black athletes were finding U of H an attractive alternative not only in football but also in basketball. The city of Houston boasted enough quality athletes in its public schools alone to produce fine football and basketball teams. Many of these athletes were black. Yeoman and Fairbanks were comfortable with that. They'd grown accustomed to coaching black athletes while at Michigan State. During the same period, Coach Yeoman crafted a new offensive formation intended to use speed and deception to offset lack of depth and subpar line play. By the mid-1960s, Yeoman, Fairbanks, and the rest of the coaching staff were creating offensive mismatches on the corners which opened up running lanes for the quarterback or the trailing halfback. The offense, labeled the Houston Veer, proved so potent that Yeoman's Houston Cougars set national rushing records and established themselves as a force to be reckoned with. The Houston Veer was adopted by the University of Texas, by the Oklahoma Sooners, and many other prominent institutions. At that time, no one could have imagined that the Veer was in fact the predecessor of the most prolific college running attack ever devised.

For Darrell Royal, the 1965, 1966, and 1967 seasons were frustrating. The Longhorns lost four games in each of those seasons. The Texas oligarchy that impacted policy and fundraising at UT-Austin was displeased. In the final game of the 1967 season, Texas lost to its bitter cross-state rival, Texas A&M, leaving Royal apoplectic. He determined that in 1968 spring ball, he was going to eliminate anyone or anything that could not totally commit to winning football games. The team would be deconstructed and reassembled no matter how painful it might be.

In *Horns, Hogs, and Nixon Coming*, Author Terry Frei provides some context for the days leading up to the December 6, 1969 encounter between number one-ranked Texas and number two-ranked Arkansas in Fayetteville. The singular impact of the 1963 national championship at Texas had enhanced the feudal system of lords and vassals, of which Darrell Royal was a willing participant. 1969 was, in retrospect, the final days of the most egregious aspect of that system. Desegregation had been too long in coming to Austin and Fayetteville. Football players at UT and Arkansas were white, almost exclusively middle class, and eager to fit into the mold established for them. Frei writes, "The Longhorns felt a mixture of fear, respect, hatred, anger, confusion, and reverence—and all of those emotions could swirl within a single player." 1969 guard Mike Dean told Frei, "You were scared to death of him (Royal). Literally scared to death of him. I don't know anybody who wasn't scared to death." Linebacker Scott Henderson, a junior in 1969, says of Coach Royal, "Some people thought he was ruthless. Some people thought he was unfair." Royal's technique of intermittent reinforcement by questioning players' manhood was difficult for young men of nineteen or twenty years old.

The UT spring practices of 1968 were brutal. Prior to spring practice, trainer Frank Medina had supervised the off-season workouts. Those had been equally brutal. Guard Bobby Mitchell told Frei, "Medina was somewhat of a henchman. He was running people off, really." There was no more charming a fellow than Coach Royal when you met him at a banquet or restaurant. He made the rounds of the tables, shaking hands with well-wishers with a broad grin. However, his practice demeanor was precisely the opposite. Frei writes, "If [the players] stayed with Royal and the Longhorns, they knew they were subject to exhausting workouts and caustic comments." Bill Zapalac, a star linebacker for the 1969 team, said, "Those 1968 spring drills were hellacious. They weeded out some of the upperclassmen. I don't know if it was intentional, but a lot of people quit." Zapalac was being charitable. His father, Willie Zapalac, was an assistant coach. All in all, some thirty players quit the team. Thirty more were injured in the drills.

One irony is that quarterback James Street missed the 1968 spring drills in order to play baseball for new Longhorn coach Augie Garrido. Had Street participated in the spring drills and gotten injured or quit in disgust, the books of Texas football history could have been different.

Assistant offensive coach Emory Bellard tinkered with the full house T-formation to take advantage of the fine running backs available on his squad. Royal was willing to roll the dice on all fronts. He was intent on identifying who was committed to playing football but also what offensive formation best suited their skill sets. As Bellard experimented, he discovered running back Steve Worster was a step too slow and running back Chris Gilbert a step too fast to execute existing Veer option plays. By moving Worster a step behind the quarterback and Gilbert and the other halfback a step back, the Veer formation became what Houston sportswriter Mickey Herskowitz labeled the Wishbone. It also became clear that Bill Bradley lacked the quickness necessary to execute at quarterback, thus leading to his replacement by James Street. Bradley was moved to defensive back. An early season tie with Coach Yeoman's Houston Cougars and a loss to Texas Tech provided the urgency to further refine UT's Wishbone attack. As a result, the Longhorns didn't lose another game the rest of the 1968 season and defeated Tennessee in the Cotton Bowl to finish 9–1–1.

A year later on December 6, 1969, a spectacle unfolded on an overcast, chilly day in Fayetteville, Arkansas. From Texas's point of view, it was the second most important game in Longhorn history, second only to the 1963 OU-Texas game which yielded Texas's first ever national championship. Arkansas was quarterbacked by a Texan—Bill Montgomery. Arkansas's fine placekicker, Bill McClard, was an Oklahoman. On the other hand, the University of Texas went to extraordinary lengths to present itself to the nation as being comprised entirely of native Texans. This wasn't true, of course. There were a handful of out-of-state players on the roster, including Freddie Steinmark of Colorado and Jim Bertelsen of Wisconsin. The University's deceptive marketing efforts were important enough that Governor Preston Smith issued Honorary Texan Certificates to each out-of-state player. The Texas athletic department had found a way to preserve Texas exceptionalism.

Arkansas coach Frank Broyles and Darrell Royal were close friends. Friendship would, however, take a back seat during this epic battle. The game became an instant classic, with Arkansas jumping out to a fourteen to nothing lead. The stadium packed full of Razorback fans were "calling the Hogs" at maximum decibels. Coach Broyles and his staff devised a defensive scheme that befuddled the Longhorns. However, the Horns fought back and with four minutes to play in the game, were trailing fourteen to eight. Coach Royal realized that even if Texas moved the ball on the ground, they would run out of time. Royal gambled. Quarterback James Street lofted a long pass to end Randy Peschel. Peschel was well-covered by a corner and a safety but the ball was thrown perfectly. Peschel made the grab over the outstretched arms of the defenders and tumbled to the ground inside the ten yard-line. Two plays later, Jim Bertelsen scored. With Happy Feller's conversion, Texas' miraculous comeback was complete and Royal's second national championship secured. President Nixon appeared on television congratulating Royal and the squad in the Texas locker room.

With the victory, Royal's Longhorns were labeled the last lily-white national championship team. And so it was. The time for desegregation of Texas and Arkansas appeared to be at hand.

Glenn Booher had been placed on the Longhorns's attack team

during the spring of 1969. That meant his practice unit would mimic the offensive attack of the next opponent during scrimmages. During this time, Booher suffered his second knee injury. That summer, he went home to Oklahoma City intent upon rehabilitating his knee and getting into shape for fall drills back in Austin. He carried with him a binder of Longhorns' offensive plays to study over the summer. All of the players on the squad had this binder. One of Booher's old high school coaches at Oklahoma City Northwest Classen, Jack Treat, was now coaching west of Oklahoma City in Clinton. Coach Treat invited Glenn to drive out to Clinton for lunch and to visit, which Booher did. The two talked football at length. Eventually, the subject turned to what Texas was doing offensively. Booher described for Treat how the Wishbone was being refined to be more effective. Finally, Booher said, "Well, coach, I have my playbook in the car and I'll show you." Treat pored over the pages with intense interest. Finally, Treat said, "Glenn, let me borrow this for a few days and I'll bring it back to you on my next trip to Oklahoma City." Booher believed Treat trustworthy and agreed. Weeks later, Coach Treat still hadn't returned Booher's playbook. In fact, Treat never returned it. When Booher returned to Austin, he was required to turn in his playbook. "I don't have it," he told the student manager. "Why not?" the manager asked. "Because I loaned it to my old high school coach and he never returned it." Coach Royal went ballistic when he heard about the incident. Booher knew that his playbook would make its way into the hands of the Oklahoma football coaching staff. And so did Darrell Royal.

The matter spelled the end of Glenn Booher's days as an active Texas Longhorn. He was never allowed to check out equipment for practice. And he never spoke to Coach Royal again.

Author Richard Pennington writes in *Breaking the Ice* that as far back as 1967 a UT student group, the Negro Association for Progress (NAP), had been picketing Memorial Stadium during football games to protest the lack of black athletes at UT. The 1967 Longhorns had struggled to another 6–4 season. An all-white group of freshmen players observed from the sidelines. When asked about the racist climate within UT's athletic department, Royal, then the head foot-ball coach and athletic director, would say, "I don't call the shots at the University of Texas." Who, then, was calling the shots? By 1969, Royal had made an enemy of Frank Erwin, which wasn't a hard thing to do. Erwin issued orders and expected them to be followed. Many others, including members of the UT faculty, had their own run-ins with Erwin. In most cases, Erwin made it so uncomfortable for them that they left UT for greener pastures. Prominent faculty member and Dean of Arts and Sciences, John Silber, resisted depart-mental changes and prompted Erwin to direct his fire at Silber, who left UT and later became president of Boston University. However, there was an irony to Erwin's behavior. Erwin, as a former protégé of the Connally/Johnson political machine, was proactive in deseg-regating all aspects of campus life including athletics. Other regents and Texas state legislators felt precisely the opposite. Royal was therefore buffeted it from all sides. Pennington cites an observation made by former Baylor assistant coach Jack Thomas: "Royal said he was going to dance with who brung him. Well, the colored boys didn't bring him."

In fact, a single black football player, linebacker Leon O'Neal, Junior, signed a letter of intent with Texas in the spring of 1968. By that time, archrival Oklahoma had approximately fifteen black football players on its roster. O'Neal, however, flunked out after his freshman year thus adding fuel to the naysayers who defended UT as being too academically demanding for blacks.

With the assassination of Martin Luther King, Junior in 1968, the racial climate on the Forty Acres heated up. Coach Royal laid low and continued to "slow play" integration. Finally, in the spring of 1969, UT signed Julius Whittier. That UT signed only one black football player smacked of tokenism to many observers. Whittier went on to start on the offensive line as a junior and played tight end as a senior. He graduated with a degree in philosophy before going on to UT Law School. It seemed that black athletes could succeed at the University of Texas after all.

The 1970 football season was another success for Royal and the

Longhorns. Powered by its Wishbone attack, UT rolled over all of its regular season opponents. A Cotton Bowl loss to Notre Dame prevented UT from winning the AP national championship; however, the final UPI coaches' poll awarded Texas its national championship prior to the bowl games. The Longhorns proudly touted their back-to-back national championship wins. By all accounts, the 1970 season represented a high point in Darrell Royal's coaching career. His reluctance to actively recruit black athletes, his barbarous practice regimen, and his penchant for disposing of young men who didn't measure up to his athletic standards represented obsolete coaching methods. Gridiron glories were to be measured by victories alone. For many of the Texas faithful and residents of the old Confederacy, that was enough.

Barry Switzer was born October 5, 1937 in Crossett, Arkansas. Crossett is near the state line with Louisiana and has a current population of about 5,000 people. The town was sixty percent white and forty percent black. Barry tragically lost his mother to suicide. His father was a bootlegger among other things and also died violently. Barry attended the flagship university of his state on a football scholarship, where he determined to pursue a career as a football coach.

By comparison, Darrell Royal was born July 6, 1924, in Hollis, Oklahoma. Hollis is near the state line with Texas and has a current population of about 2,000 people. Hollis was sixty seven percent white, thirteen percent black, with the remainder Latinos and various races. Darrell lost his mother to illness while he was an infant. His father was an industrious man but also a serial bridegroom who was married five times. There was little time for Burley Ray Royal to nurture his kids. Darrell attended the flagship university of his state on a football scholarship, where he also determined to pursue a career as a football coach.

Barry Switzer and Darrell Royal each won three national championships during their respective careers at Oklahoma and Texas. Each has subsequently been inducted into the National College Football Hall of Fame. If growing up in relative poverty under difficult family circumstances affected the two of them, it could be said that the wounds were hidden behind steely resolve and the relentless pursuit of accomplishment. Although Royal was some thirteen years older than Switzer, they both emerged from the same post-war environment. Each was married and produced three children, two boys and a girl each. The similarities between the two men ended there.

Switzer arrived on the OU campus in the spring of 1966, after being hired as offensive coordinator by new OU head coach, Jim Mackenzie. Mackenzie's coaching staff included Chuck Fairbanks, up from the University of Houston, to be defensive secondary coach. The 1966 season saw Oklahoma post a 6–4 record. Still, there was a feeling of optimism as Oklahoma had beaten Texas eighteen to nine. It was Oklahoma's first victory over Darrell Royal's Longhorns since 1957. When Mackenzie died suddenly of a heart attack, the OU Board of Regents and Athletic Department scrambled to find a suitable replacement and sustain OU's progress. Chuck Fairbanks won the job. Fairbanks was older and more experienced than others on the staff. He assured his employers that he would continue to build upon the progress made in 1966. The 1967 Sooners did so in grand style, finishing with a 10–1 record. They lost only to Texas, nine to seven, but defeated Tennessee in the Orange Bowl. The 1968 and 1969 OU teams produced four-loss seasons, including losses to Texas. Early in the 1970 season, OU was upset by Oregon State in Norman. After that game, Switzer suggested that they make a mid-season change from the Houston Veer to the Wishbone. It was a shocking suggestion. OU had to play Texas in just two weeks. The first order of business was to sell the idea to OU quarterback Jack Mildren of Abilene, Texas. Mildren reluctantly agreed to give it a try. Even though the Sooners employed their awkward version of the Wishbone and lost badly to Texas, forty-one to nine, OU finished the season with a 7–4 record. Better days lay ahead.

Other major football powers were likewise instituting the Wishbone formation. Bear Bryant and his Alabama Crimson Tide found the offense productive and used it to secure national championships. As with all innovations, it would take time for defensive gurus to develop an antidote for the formation's potency.

Greg Pruitt was a diminutive wide receiver who had been recruited to Oklahoma from Houston's B.C. Elmore High School. Pruitt was among the first of many black athletes to be recruited out of the Houston area by Fairbanks's staff. Pruitt was fast—and a fast talker. No one in the Oklahoma locker room expected the five foot nine Pruitt to contribute much to Oklahoma's Veer offense. However, after they converted to the Wishbone, Pruitt was moved to halfback.

In the fall of 1971, OU's experiment with the Wishbone took a stunning turn. The flying Sooners demolished its first three opponents, including Southern Cal, before meeting the Longhorns in Dallas. The Longhorns had disposed of UCLA, Texas Tech, and Oregon earlier in the season in route to the Dallas match-up. Texas came into the game ranked number three while OU was ranked number eight. Each team's version of the Wishbone was piling up points, yards, and victories. At halftime, OU led thirty-one to twenty-one. It seemed as if neither side could defend the other's ground attack. Scoring continued at a torrid pace in the second half. Greg Pruitt scored three touchdowns himself. He logged 216 yards rushing in twenty carries for an average gain of 10.8 yards per carry. The final score was Oklahoma forty-eight, Texas twenty-seven.

A deflated Texas squad lost the next week to Arkansas while OU rolled ahead toward its traditional Thanksgiving rivalry game against Nebraska. Both teams were marvelous in every way. Sportswriters dubbed the contest the Game of the Century. Nebraska's I-formation attack featuring Johnny Rodgers, Jeff Kinney, and Jerry Tagge was virtually unstoppable. Pruitt was injured and didn't play in the game. The game became an offensive shootout; the last team that had the ball emerged the victor, which was Nebraska, who won thirty-five to thirty-one. Oklahoma went on to defeat Auburn and Heisman Trophy winner Pat Sullivan in the Sugar Bowl while Nebraska handled Alabama in the Orange Bowl on their way to the national championship. Penn State defeated Texas in the Cotton Bowl. In unusual circumstances, the Big Eight Conference secured the first, second, and third ranked positions in the final AP poll. They were Nebraska, Oklahoma, and Colorado in that order.

The Sooners had taken the offensive concept devised at the University of Texas and refined it into the most prolific offense college football has ever known. Ironically, they accomplished this by adding speed from the contributions of black Texas athletes who UT did not recruit. Oklahoma averaged 472.4 rushing yards per game in 1971 and 44.5 points per game. They now had the competitive advantage.

DAYS OF SORROW

The manager of a local band called Shiva's Headband, stepped out behind the south Austin dive bar to relieve himself between sets. In the moonlight, he could make out an old multi-story brick building with high steel casement windows. He sensed a certain foreboding about it. That didn't prevent him and a couple of buddies from searching for a way to get in. Finally they found an open garage door. They pulled up a car and shone its headlights into the place. What they saw was a cavernous shell with brick walls and exposed steel girders for roof support. There was only a concrete floor below. This place would make a cool music venue, the band manager thought, bad acoustics and all. A little investigation the next day revealed that the building was an abandoned National Guard armory hidden behind the Skating Palace roller rink on Barton Springs Road. "Cheap rent is what made it possible for us to turn that old drafty armory into the Armadillo World Headquarters," said partner Max Smith. The "Dillo" became something far beyond a local honky tonk. It was a communal residence for thousands of countercultural residents of Austin. Most

119

of the help at the Dillo were unpaid volunteers. They just wanted to be a part of the grand adventure. On August 7, 1970, the Dillo opened for business. There were slow nights and packed ones over the months and years ahead. People found out about the music programs from word-of-mouth and from inexpensively produced show posters tacked to poles all over south Austin and the University of Texas. The posters were designed by skilled artists who often donated their services. Jim Franklin was the most prominent of these. Franklin's posters generally reflected a psychedelic theme complete with at least one smiling armadillo with a joint in its mouth. The popularity of the Dillo was unplanned and unexpected. It became a national mecca for a generation of hippies, just as the Fillmore in San Francisco had been. Talent agents contacted the Dillo's management for bookings. Unlike most venues, the Armadillo World Headquarters didn't limit itself to any particular genre of music. They booked blues musicians like B. B. King, country artists like Willie Nelson, and rock-and-rollers who made it a permanent home. Everyone was welcome to perform and to listen. The headliners commanded top dollar and while the Dillo could seat 1,500 patrons, on the big nights there weren't nearly enough seats. When that happened, there were ample carpet remnants for folks to sit or lie on. The music and the pot smoke wafted up and among the steel beams and created an eerie, surreal vibe. People loved it. However, there was a complicating aspect of the club's operation—it never operated like a business. Cash was the only method of payment in those days, and it flowed in and out. There were no books to speak of. The local owners didn't make any money. It didn't seem to matter. Smoking pot was acceptable at the Dillo. Somehow the place was never raided, possibly because the local authorities knew regular visitors included high state government officials from Congress Avenue, professors from UT, and prominent business tycoons. The Armadillo World Headquarters became something far beyond live music and communal living. It signified freedom.

Willie Nelson found the place so welcoming that he and his band left Nashville to take up residence in Austin. Their move turned out to be a God send. It gave Willie the freedom to perform his own way and to sing his own songs. The result was the distinctive Austin sound. Its birthplace was the abandoned National Guard armory hidden behind a roller skating rink.

At the end of the 1971 football season and before UT's Gator Bowl game against Penn State, Emory Bellard resigned from the Texas coaching staff to become head coach at Texas A&M. This stunning development meant that A&M would develop its own potent version of the Wishbone offense. Additionally, UT would be forced to adjust to the challenges created by an offensive innovation that was created on its campus and had spread nationwide. Darrell Royal was seething in silence. Moving from job to job was a part of the college coaching profession. Darrell, however, valued loyalty. After all, he plucked Bellard out of San Angelo Central High School. In any event, opportunity knocked for Emory Bellard and he answered.

Coach Bellard's first two seasons at A&M produced sub-par results. Aggie fans were forced to be patient. However, by 1974 the Aggies had recruited the speed necessary to succeed with the Wishbone. Finally, in 1975 Texas A&M defeated Texas for the first time since 1967. The following season, 1976, A&M drilled the Longhorns on their home field, twenty-seven to three. The 1976 season would prove to be a turning point for Darrell Royal's coaching career.

On June 21, 1999, a middle-aged man with a history of mental illness died of a heart attack at age 53. At the time of his death, he was residing in his hometown of Denton, Texas. For a decade or more, the man had been homeless and roaming the dark streets and alleys of Dallas. It was a sad ending to a troubled life. In his youth, the man had been a football star at Denton High School before committing to play for Darrell Royal's Texas Longhorns in the spring of 1963. That fall, the Longhorns would win their first ever national championship. The glorious gridiron events of 1963 had emboldened Coach Royal. At New York's National Football Foundation convention, before the largest press conference Royal had ever seen, he received the MacArthur Bowl in recognition of his Longhorns as the nation's college football national champions. The trophy was handed to Coach Royal by General Douglas A. MacArthur. Royal, always attracted to celebrities, could scarcely believe his newfound status. The coach's photograph appeared with his players on the covers of sports magazines. He was heavily sought as a dinner speaker. He and Edith were added to the A-list of invitees to elite Dallas and Houston social events.

It was in this environment that the kid from Denton found himself in the fall of 1963. His name was Gary Shaw. In the fall of 1972, long after Shaw had departed the Forty Acres, he wrote a book about his UT experience that would set collegiate football on its ear. The title of the book was *Meat on the Hoof.* In it, Shaw scathingly indicted the University of Texas football program. He was especially critical of Coach Royal, who he considered a tyrant. There had never been a book like it. Shaw's central thesis was that Royal purposely set about to destroy players' sense of self and replace it with sense of group.

Now, some forty-two years after publication of *Meat on the Hoof,* one might concede that Shaw was a wounded soul with a tortured view of the world. But the book sold over 350,000 copies. It got the attention of people who care about the college game and the young men who played it. The book profoundly affected the way Texas football and Coach Royal were viewed by the public. Royal would spend the rest of his career attempting to remove its stain from his reputation. Had there actually been physical and emotional abuse along with academic fraud at UT during the 1960s, it would all be extinguished over time not by repentance but by the transformational impact of integration, scholarship limitations, and fierce recruiting competition.

Coach Royal was granted academic tenure in 1965 by UT Chancellor Harry Ransom. This was a way of fending off attempts by the University of Oklahoma and perhaps other universities at luring Royal away from Austin. There were vocal protests from UT faculty over Ransom's action. If anyone doubted the gravity of Longhorn football before Ransom's actions, they now had been convinced otherwise.

Marian Royal Kazen's life as a mother and politician's wife in the Washington, D.C. suburbs was increasingly miserable. The social and political climate of Washington left her suffocated and angry. Her husband's ambitions seemed to be the important thing. The only thing. They summoned up resentment of her father's singular focus on his coaching career. Marian understood her duty. It was to be seen and not heard, just as her mother was comfortable doing in Austin. Caring for two small boys dominated her days. Parenting was not in her nature, although she was a dutiful mother. Marian was an artist at heart. She harbored strong political views which were radical in nature. She abhorred how President Nixon handled the Vietnam War and believed the United States should withdraw immediately. Anti-war demonstrations were frequent events in the nation's capital. Her instincts told her to take it to the streets.

Mack Royal penned a feature story for an online publication in Austin called *The End of Austin*, which was posted on May 18, 2013. The story, "Spirits of the Weird," was written in third person with Eddy Franklin as the protagonist. (The name Eddy Franklin was an alias for Mack Royal.) Mack wrote, "He (Franklin) and his sister shared a wild streak. Where it came from they did not know." It came as no surprise, then, when Mack received a telephone call from Marian in 1971 in which she confided that she was at her breaking point. She told Mack, "I've shaved my eyebrows off so I don't have to go to any more political dinners. If I don't get out of here, I'm going to go crazy."

Marian eventually left Chic Kazen. She took only her clothes and her babies in the car and headed for Austin. Once home, Darrell and Edith bought a home for her and her boys. When the divorce proceedings got underway in earnest, the matter turned adversarial. Chic sought custody of his sons. Chic was a skilled attorney. He knew that in order to prevail over the natural mother of minor children, he would have to allege that Marian was an unfit parent.

Marian's anguish intensified when it became clear Darrell and Edith were ambivalent about the divorce proceedings.

Once back in Austin, Marian returned to her life's calling through her art and radical politics. She was commissioned by Eddie Wilson down at the Armadillo World Headquarters to paint a mural on the wall of the club. Not unexpectedly, she found herself spending time at the Armadillo World Headquarters among countercultural friends and fellow activists. According to Mack, Marian attended a campus rally featuring members of the radical Black Panthers. Apparently, she spent the rest of the night with the visiting revolutionaries. Sometime later she confided to Mack that she intended to move to Chicago and marry one of the Black Panthers. None of these plans would come to fruition. Tragedy intervened. In March of 1973, Marian was in a rush to pick up her older son Christian from nursery school. She was afraid she would be late for a lunch date with her former sister-in-law. With the two boys in the car, a UT shuttle bus broadsided Marian's car. For weeks, she lay in a coma. Edith could barely stand to see her beautiful daughter hooked up to life support machines. Darrell visited his daughter daily. On April 11, 1973, she passed away.

Edith Royal describes the sorrow of those days in a book she co-authored, *DKR, The Royal Family Scrapbook*. She had good friends upon whom to lean. She enrolled in a grief counseling program. She learned over time to put one foot in front of the other and direct her efforts into something fulfilling. She found comfort through charity work.

Mack was struggling with his own personal demons. At the age of twenty-one, he married Madeline, the daughter of a prominent university research scientist, in 1968. Madeline's parents were divorced and Madeline's mother wielded great influence over her daughter. The mother-in-law didn't care for Mack. In fact, Mack didn't care for himself. Mack was leading his life in a whimsical haze. For a time, Mack, Madeline, and their baby boy, Sammy, lived with Madeline's mother in Las Vegas, New Mexico, where she accepted a teaching position at New Mexico Highlands University. Mack enjoyed the slow pace of New Mexico life. The area had a mystical quality that appealed to him. Mack, however, lacked direction. This took its toll on the marriage. Inevitably, Mack and Madeline divorced. Mack's online magazine article referred to the experience this way: "[Franklin] married a psycho instead of a debutante." Darrell and Edith arranged for Madeline and their grandson to move into the house they had purchased for Marian. It seemed that every value, every sense of discipline and ambition that Coach Royal manifested throughout his coaching career had been rejected by his own children.

David Wade, the youngest of the Royal children, became the focus of Darrell's affection. David attended a private school in west Austin, Saint Stephens, and had also spent some time in New York as a music student. Now, at the age of twenty in 1973, David was living in the house that had been originally purchased for his sister. David was in the stage of his life where every day was an adventure. By all accounts, David exhibited his father's charisma. He also enjoyed many male friends and was a leader among them no matter what mischief they got into.

In *Breaking the Ice*, Richard Pennington refers to Coach Royal's tardy recruitment of black athletes as a "sin of omission." However, by the spring of 1971, three black athletes had signed letters of intent with the Longhorns. Roosevelt Leaks, a high school senior, was joined by two junior college transfers, Donald Ealy and Howard Shaw. Additionally, Royal had taken a small step toward desegregating his coaching staff by hiring a black part time defensive coach, Alvin Matthews. Matthews was UT's first black coach in any sport. Matthews's main task was to recruit black athletes and in so doing, dispel any notion of racism on the Forty Acres. Oddly, in the spring of 1972, not a single black athlete signed with Texas. The mass exodus of black athletes out of state continued unabated.

If the release of *Meat on the Hoof* in 1972 was not sufficiently negative publicity, two Associated Press writers, Jack Keever and Robert Heard, obtained Coach Royal's approval to interview his football players and coaching staff as a part of their research into racism allegations within the Texas program. The five-part series was devastating. Each of the few black team members were interviewed by the writers. All expressed dissatisfaction with the racial climate in Austin. It was a historical fact that Austin had a long history of segregation in housing, education, and employment. Some of the players who gave interviews later apologized to Coach Royal, but by then the damage was done. Even Roosevelt Leaks, who was a star running back with a professional playing career ahead of him, told the writers he perceived sullen racism among his white teammates. When the subject came up years later between Royal's biographer, Jimmy Banks, and Coach Royal, Royal said, "If I had anything to be regretful about as far as blacks were concerned, that was it—I just wasn't concerned soon enough about trying to help them." In 1973, Coach Royal was still perplexed by the issue of race. Black athletes didn't need his help. They wanted his respect.

THE PURGE

Some have written that Royal truly believed with regard to the 1972 OU–Texas game that OU had been spying on Texas practices leading up to the Red River Shootout that year. The Longhorns had fashioned a fine record in 1972, losing only to OU, twenty-seven to nothing. Texas subsequently defeated Bear Bryant's Crimson Tide in the Cotton Bowl, earning a number three finish in the final AP rankings.

It was true, in fact, that speculation about questionable tactics was rampant regarding Oklahoma—but the issue wasn't spying. Coach Chuck Fairbanks resigned abruptly in order to take the head coaching position with the New England Patriots. OU quickly elevated offensive coordinator Barry Switzer to head coach at the start of the 1973 season. The NCAA, it was reported, had been investigating the OU football program. They were focusing on allegations that Galveston Ball High School quarterback Kerry Jackson and a teammate, Mike Phillips, did not qualify to enroll at OU based upon the applicable academic standards of high school grades and test scores. It was alleged that these students' high school transcripts had been altered. These allegations resulted in Oklahoma being sanctioned and placed on probation by the NCAA. Among the sanctions were forfeiture of any 1972 victories in which one of the involved players participated, no bowl game appearances in the 1973–1974 seasons, and no television appearances from 1974 to 1975.

Coach Royal may have felt vindicated for his suspicions that OU's recruiting efforts in the state of Texas were conducted outside the rules. In any event, OU was successfully recruiting Texas's finest black high school athletes—and its white ones as well. Wendell Mosley was hired as OU's first black assistant coach in 1972. Mosley came to Norman from Houston's B. C. Elmore High School, Greg Pruitt's alma mater. The 1972 recruiting class at OU included Jackson, Phillips, and a supremely talented running back named Joe Washington from Port Arthur, Texas. Kerry Jackson would become OU's first black quarterback. It would be years before Texas would consider recruiting a black quarterback. The NCAA had just authorized freshmen to participate in varsity sports, thus opening the door for Kerry Jackson to make an immediate impact for the Sooners.

During the 1972 season, Coach Switzer occasionally substituted Jackson for starter and senior quarterback Dave Robertson. In the first four games of 1972, Jackson was the team's third leading rusher. Oklahoma finished the season 11–1, defeating Penn State in the Sugar Bowl. Three of those victories were later forfeited because of game participation by Jackson and or Mike Phillips. In April, 1973, Jackson and Phillips were declared ineligible to play for OU for the remainder of that year. Both young men elected to stay at OU. The door was open, however, for Steve Davis—an obscure squad man from Sallisaw, Oklahoma—to start at quarterback in the powerful Oklahoma Wishbone. Over the next three seasons, Davis would lead the Sooners to a record of 32–1–1 and back-to-back national championships in 1974 and 1975. *Sports Illustrated* featured a cover article in 1974 titled "The Best Team You'll Never See," referring to OU's television ban that season.

Some observers say that after his daughter Marian's death in 1973, Darrell Royal's heart wasn't in coaching football anymore. However, there was no speculation that he would quit coaching as there had been after Reggie Grob's practice-induced death in 1961. Quitting over Marian's death was counterintuitive. He needed to stay busy more than ever. His competitive drive and natural instincts led him to double down on winning. With Barry Switzer taking over at OU, the competitive tension between Royal's alma mater and his Longhorns changed dramatically. Both coaches were charismatic, intense, and imminently quotable. Switzer's declarations were decidedly genuine and disarming. After Oklahoma defeated Texas fifty-two to thirteen in 1973, he told reporters gathered in the steamy Cotton Bowl locker room, "When you beat the University of Texas, I don't care what your won-lost record is, it's the greatest day of your life!" That was as fine a tribute to Coach Royal and the Longhorns as anyone could give. The Longhorns won every regular season game on its schedule except for the blowout loss to OU. Nebraska defeated Texas in the Cotton Bowl Classic, nineteen to three.

Sooner Century, the history of Oklahoma football, states, "In the 70s, when black players were still rare at Texas and Arkansas, Switzer had black co-captains, black quarterbacks, and black assistant coaches. Switzer was likewise fond of saying, "It isn't the x's and o's, it's the Jimmys and Joes."

Coach Royal reinvigorated his coaching career in the spring of 1974, when Earl Cambpell, the "Tyler Rose", signed a letter of intent with UT. Interestingly, Oklahoma believed they would sign Campbell but Campbell's mother found the white Texas recruiter, Ken Dabbs, to have just the right amount of down-home fatherliness to reassure her about her son. Dabbs would leave the Campbell home in Tyler and while standing on the front porch, he'd turn around and say, "Now remember, a little Dabbs will do ya!"

In 1974, Texas found itself twenty point underdogs to the Sooners prompted by an early season loss to Texas Tech. The AP poll ranked Oklahoma number two behind Ohio State. While the Longhorns had Earl Campbell in the lineup, Oklahoma countered with brothers Lee Roy and Dewey Selmon on the defensive line. The game was played at a far different pace than the previous year's contest. Missed opportunities plagued both teams, with OU leading only seven to three at the half. The final score was OU sixteen, Texas thirteen. Later in the season, Woody Hayes's Buckeyes would stumble against Michigan State and allow Oklahoma to ascend to number one. OU went on to post an unblemished record of 11–0 but was banned from bowl participation as part of its probation. Regardless, OU finished first in the AP poll and claimed its fourth national championship. Auburn defeated the Longhorns twenty-seven to three in the Gator Bowl. At that point, OU had defeated Texas four years in a row and had won 29 straight games.

Spring recruiting in 1975 provided Oklahoma with an opportunity to capitalize on its recent good fortune. It did so by recruiting a monstrous freshman class—seventeen Texas players, including the Lone Star State's three best running backs, the best quarterback, the best linebacker, and two of the best defensive linemen. In an attempt to slow down OU's pilfering of Texas players, Texas led the Southwest Conference in successfully passing NCAA legislation to limit the number of in-person visits a school's coaches could make to a recruit. Royal said it was a cost-cutting measure, but observers knew otherwise. The recruiting magician, Barry Switzer, and his assistants were undaunted.

If Coach Royal and Coach Switzer were among the most quotable in all of sports, those reputations would be enhanced by the blood feud that commenced a full eight months before the Red River Shootout. In *Annual Madness*, Bill Cromartie writes, "Royal was fed up. He had, in the past, made statements giving rise to strong inferences that Oklahoma used illegal and unethical recruiting methods regarding Texas school boy talent. The Texas faithful were understandably searching for an explanation—any explanation—for having lost to their archrival for five straight years. To their minds, the Sooner raids of Texas high school talent were tantamount to cattle-rustling. Switzer, the quotable coach, retorted, "Certain coaches (referring to Royal) should do more recruiting and less listening to country and western guitar pickers." The last straw for many Texas fans was when Oklahoma was picked as the preseason favorite to repeat as national champions in 1975. Texas was expected to field a strong team and finish in the top ten.

The Sooners were up and down early in the season but like all great teams, they found a way to win. The OU–Texas game was yet another spectacle. The game was played in brutally hot, humid, October weather. In a contest this intense, mistakes can make the difference. For the second year in a row, there was no television coverage due to OU's probation. Fumbles, penalties, and trick plays were abundant that October afternoon. OU managed to escape with the victory, twenty-four to seventeen. Those close to Royal said later that he had been desperate to win the game. His competitive spirit made it gut-wrenching for him to lose to his old school five times in a row. The Oklahoma recruiting bonanza continued unabated south of the Red River. Royal and his army of supporters were looking for a rallying point. The following October, 1976, they found one.

The day before the 1976 OU–Texas game, an article ran in *The Daily Oklahoman* newspaper that accused OU of spying on Texas practices. According to Bill Cromartie, "The accusation against OU was made public Friday by head coach Darrell Royal, who said he would pay Switzer and the alleged spy, Lonnie Williams, 10,000 dollars each to donate to their favorite charities if they would take lie detector tests to prove their innocence." Royal denied that he was breaking the story to give his team and fans an incendiary boost. There was a good deal of back-and-forth between Switzer and Royal in the hours leading up to the game as a result of the allegation.

OU came into the game with a 4–0 record and ranked number three behind Michigan and Pittsburgh. The Longhorns lost their season opener to Boston College. In the Red River Shootout, the two teams performed as if they had been emotionally drained by the ongoing scandal. Texas only scored two field goals off the foot of their outstanding placekicker, Russell Erxleben. OU didn't score at all until there was a minute thirty-eight seconds left in the game. At that point Horace Ivory, yet another outstanding black athlete from Texas, looped around left end from the one-yard line for a touchdown. The ensuing conversion snap sailed high, denying OU a game-winning extra point. For the third time in series history and for the first time in thirty-nine years, the fierce rivals tied. Texas won only three of its remaining seven games to finish at 5–5–1. On December 4 in Austin, the Longhorns defeated Arkansas twenty-nine to twelve in what would be Darrell K Royal's last game as a coach.

It's difficult to identify the tipping point that led Darrell Royal to resign as head coach at the University of Texas. His life story reflected great joy and great sorrow. Darrell survived a difficult childhood. He survived the Dust Bowl, the Great Depression, and World War II. He found the love of his life, Edith Thomason, while he was still in high school. He lost his only daughter, Marian, to a 1973 car accident. He won 219 games at UT; he won or shared eleven Southwest Conference titles and three national championships. He established a legacy at the University of Texas for the ages. And he was only fifty-two years old.

Darrell understood that if he were to also resign as athletic director, some would speculate that he'd been fired. While he had no particular interest in continuing as AD, he maintained those on-going responsibilities after resigning as football coach. He assured long-standing and loyal assistants like Leon Manley and Mike Campbell that he would take care of them in the coaching transition.

When Father Fred Bomar passed away in 2010, the *Austin Statesman-American* ran a feature story under the title, "Monsignor Fred Bomar was an Austin Fixture." He certainly was that. Upon arriving at St. Peter the Apostle Catholic Church in southeast Austin in 1969 as parish priest, he immediately became enthralled with the Texas Longhorns football team. He had every reason to feel that way. In Texas, football was close to a religious experience. Additionally, the Longhorns won a national championship in 1969 in the wake of the Fayetteville spectacle against the Hogs while President Nixon was in attendance. That national championship was followed by a second national championship in 1970. The newspaper article called Bomar an avid Longhorn supporter who for a time was also chaplain for the Texas House of Representatives. UT head coach David McWilliams said of Bomar, "He was also well-known among University of Texas athletes as a man who was always around but never in the way." Athletic Director DeLoss Dodds said at the time that Father Bomar had been a big part of the University. "He was a friend to everybody and a special friend to us." By all accounts, Father Bomar was a fine man who relished establishing relationships outside the parish family.

An insider at UT shared revealing details about Father Bomar. Apparently, Bomar embraced by Frank Erwin as a personal friend and confidante. It is said that Father Bomar and Erwin spent many evenings discussing Erwin's efforts to mold the University to his liking. A priest's gift is to be a good listener. Bomar was certainly willing to listen to Erwin. As a political protégé of Governor John Connally, who was in office from 1963 to 1969—and by association, a protégé of Lyndon Johnson—Erwin managed to get himself appointed to the UT Board of Regents. That prestigious role began in 1963 and lasted twelve years until 1975. Erwin was Board Chairman from 1966 to 1971. Erwin didn't see his task as building consensus on policy matters. Rather, he viewed himself as the dictatorial chief operating officer of the University. The university president, the faculty, and the student body could all be damned. In 1967, he was the principal architect of the University of Texas System, which was created to unify a number of regional educational institutions. The result was an aggregation of twelve component educational institutions with a staggering system budget and central administration. Erwin made sure that the University of Texas–Austin received the lion's share of the state educational budget.

Erwin's imposition of his will upon the university was marked by continuous controversy. He demanded and commanded complete control over university decision-making. Some viewed Erwin as a megalomaniac. As long as he held the powers of the purse, the proxies of Governor Connally, and even in some cases of the President of the United States, he was virtually invincible. As early as 1964, spurred on by Lyndon Johnson's landslide victory over Barry Goldwater, Erwin attracted notoriety by unilaterally firing university administrators and faculty that did not comply with his explicit instructions.

It began when he fired the university comptroller. By 1966, Erwin's zealous exercise of power had reached its zenith. He personally confronted students on campus who were protesting against the Vietnam War. He likewise harassed left-leaning faculty members for expressing their views. The conservative Texas legislature down the street from the Forty Acres applauded Erwin's provocations, believing they were being supportive of LBJ. When Erwin floated the notion of demolishing Memorial Stadium in order to make room for the new LBJ Presidential Library across the street to the north, Coach Royal reacted. Erwin was a formidable foe. Royal had only one avenue and that was to appeal to LBJ personally. This he did; Memorial Stadium stayed. But Erwin never forgot when Royal pulled rank on him. Incredibly, in a 1974 attempt to financially suffocate the student newspaper, *The Daily Texan*, Erwin declared, "We do not fund what we do not control." Coach Royal observed all of this from a distance. He was reminded of Dana X. Bible's admonition not to go near the State Capitol. Erwin, however, wasn't at the Capitol. He was only a short walk from Royal's office in the Texas Tower. Further, Royal was powerless to prevent Father Bomar from intruding into his football practices and locker room. What he told his players and what his players told Bomar were no doubt repeated to Erwin over cocktails. Royal was clearly vulnerable to Erwin as a result of his failure to pursue integration of sports and particularly football on the UT campus. For a Catholic priest working with a devotee of Johnson's Civil Rights Act of 1964, Royal's position was precarious indeed.

Coach Mike Campbell played college football at Ole Miss before embarking on his coaching career in Mississippi high schools. Darrell Royal discovered him while Campbell was coaching at Vicksburg, the historic Civil War battleground city. Coach Royal was the head coach at Mississippi State when he asked Campbell to join his coaching staff in 1955 as the MSU defensive coordinator. The two complemented each other so well that Campbell followed Royal to the University of Washington for the 1956 season before packing up once again for the long drive from Seattle to Austin. Over the next twenty seasons, Campbell developed into Royal's most loyal and trusted lieutenant. He was in charge of the Longhorn defense. Royal had actually been a better defensive back than a quarterback in his college days, so he valued Campbell's perceptive insights and teaching abilities. It was an open secret that Mike Campbell should and would succeed Royal as head coach of the Longhorns. It was assumed that current UT President Lorene Rogers would defer judgment on football matters to the Athletics Council and that the Athletics Council of which Royal was a member would defer to the wishes of the iconic coach. However, there were other forces at work. In hindsight, it seems clear that Frank Erwin thought Royal's decision-making days were over. Besides, there was a suitable alternative. Fred Akers was the head coach of the University of Wyoming. Prior to his two seasons in Laramie, he was an offensive assistant to Coach Royal from 1966 through 1974. What is known, however, is that Royal was very unhappy when Akers was selected as his successor. The issue for Erwin may not have been Akers's abilities as a coach. It might have been that he simply wasn't who Royal anointed as his successor. In any event, Akers compiled a record over ten seasons, from 1977 to 1986, which would have been considered successful at most institutions. He simply failed to replicate Coach Royal's charisma, drive, and sterling success. When Akers was hired against Royal's wishes, Mike Campbell retired from coaching. Campbell held Texas administrative posts over the next twenty years of his working life and up until his death in 1998.

Over the next two decades, Coach Royal never felt completely comfortable with the UT football program. The period of mediocrity was frustrating for most Texas fans. Royal continued to meet his obligations as athletic director for a time. The Akers era had begun well enough. The 1977 Longhorns finished eleven-one and won every regular season game before losing to Notre Dame in the Cotton Bowl, thirty-eight to ten. Darrell Royal must have experienced a bittersweet moment when the athlete that saved his career, Earl Campbell, won the 1977 Heisman Trophy with Coach Akers at his side in New York.

Royal was feeling uncomfortable and marginalized in the

workplace. He never liked going to stuffy meetings, study sessions, or audit reviews. Royal was a football man. Always had been. Over time, he began to sense that some of his duties were being shifted off of his desk. Something was afoot.

Bill Ellington was a very successful high school football coach, most prominently at Garland High School in the suburbs of Dallas and for a single season at Amarillo Tascosa. As was Royal's habit, he searched out the most dynamic, successful high school coaches in the State of Texas to join his staff. He had valid reasons. Texas was a huge state and recruiting over so many schools was so daunting that he needed assistant coaches who already had good relationships established in various parts of the State. Hence he plucked Ellington out of the high school ranks to join his UT staff in 1959. The new assistants he invited to come to Austin were good recruiters. That was top priority. In a 2013 article, UT Sports Information Director Bill Little wrote, "When it came to recruiting, the World War II vet (Ellington) could reach back to his farming days growing up in Quinlan, Texas, and charm moms and pops and instill confidence in young high school players like the ones he had coached to great success at various stops across Texas. If he hadn't been a football coach, Ellington could have made a good living as a country lawyer or politician." A Texas fan in 2013 could easily read between the lines.

Darrell Royal valued loyalty more than any other quality. Coaching football was a high risk profession. You needed to trust the man next to you. When Royal left Mississippi State, he secured the job for his college teammate and coaching assistant, Wade Walker, after whom he had named his youngest son. When he left the University of Washington, he secured the job for another college teammate and friend, Jim Owens. When Royal figured out that he was playing Caesar to Ellington's Brutus, he knew it was time to go. Years later, Royal told a writer, "I had an assistant that had a paddle for every ass." Sure enough, Bill Ellington was quietly selected to replace Royal as athletic director. Somewhere Frank Erwin was smiling.

EMPIRE

The Barton Creek census tract in west Austin is the wealthiest census tract in the state of Texas. How did it earn that distinction? From its beginning in the 1980s, the Texas overlords envisioned it that way. For the Texas gentry, living near the lavish Barton Creek Club and Resort meant rubbing elbows with the politically powerful and financially secure white elites of the state.

Social histories suggest it often happens this way. As Robin Waterfield writes in her study of the Roman Empire, *Taken from the Flood*, the original city state was ruled by an oligarchy of fabulously wealthy families. Often the best way to increase that tremendous wealth was by plundering the spoils from victories. The families perpetuated their oligarchy in that their prominence and wealth offered opportunities for influencing public policy. There were no hereditary ranks; power and prestige were precious commodities to be cultivated and preserved. That was Rome. And it was also the enclave of Austin's Barton Creek community.

Today, the Omni Barton Creek Resort and Spa trumpets its

history in all of its promotional materials. As they put it, "Omni Barton Creek Resort and Spa began with the goal of turning the beauty of 4,000 acres of untamed wilderness into one of the most sought after resort destinations in Texas. With the aid of former Governor John Connally and former Lieutenant Governor Ben Barnes, a joint venture was created with Kindred and Company to lay the foundation for the Barton Creek development in June of 1985. Two years later, the resort opened." Barnes, who had years earlier fallen victim to the Sharpsburg Bank scandal, had been a political fixer in Texas and to some degree the same in Washington, D.C. There were other prominent Texans interested in the Barton Creek development as well.

Robert Rowling earned his degree from UT–Austin and his law degree from Southern Methodist University. In 1972, he went to work for his father's oil company, Tana Oil and Gas. In 1989, Texaco purchased Tana for 476 million dollars, which led the younger Rowling to organize TRT Holdings. TRT then purchased Omni Hotels for 500 million dollars and Gold's Gym for 180 million. Rowling served as a regent for the University of Texas system until February, 2009, when he abruptly resigned over a disputed board decision. As of March 2012, Rowling's estimated net worth was 4.8 billion dollars and he was ranked as the sixty-sixth richest person in the United States. He is, as one might suspect, a conservative Republican and a major supporter of Karl Rove's American Crossroads PAC. Rove is an Austin resident. The Barton Creek Club and Resort is now considered Omni property. Ownership is in KSL Capital Partners, along with other elite resorts such as The Belfry and California's Squaw Valley Ski Resort. KSL is a private equity firm of which Rowling is likely an investor.

When the vision for the Barton Creek development was being bandied about in corporate board rooms in the 1980s, Jim Bob Moffett became the front man for the group. Moffett seemed suitable for the ambitious and somewhat controversial real estate play. After all, Moffett was a notorious hard charger. He played tackle for Darrell Royal's Longhorns from 1959 through 1961.

Darrell Royal landed in Austin to assume control of the UT football program in 1957. Moffett was among the first to catch the young coach's eye. At the time, Royal was barely a decade older than the young men in his charge. Coach Royal had a vision of gridiron glories that resonated with Jim Bob Moffett. He too, was an energetic, hard-driving dreamer. Moffett was the son of an oilfield roustabout who grew up in Houma, Louisiana. When his parents divorced, Jim Bob's mother took him and his sister to live in Houston, where she worked as a credit clerk. Jim Bob bagged groceries, delivered newspapers, pumped gas, and sold shoes. Even in those demanding 1950s, Jim Bob was active in the Boy Scouts and a member of the National Honor Society. He demonstrated at an early age a drive rarely seen—except in someone with a similar background. Someone like Darrel K Royal.

When Jim Bob arrived on the Forty Acres with a full football scholarship, he unpacked drive and ambition along with his suitcase. Years later, in 1990, Moffett's biographers called Darrell Royal Jim Bob's mentor. The relationship was much more than that of player and coach. It was a collaboration of dreams. They understood each other. They needed each other. Their relationship would last a lifetime.

While Jim Bob was playing offensive tackle for the Longhorns, he was also excelling in his chosen discipline, geology. He was proud of earning the highest scholastic average among 1961 senior football players. After graduating from UT, Moffett returned to his home state of Louisiana to begin a career in the oil patch. He started at the bottom and worked on oil rigs. His business future would eventually match his dreams.

McMoran Oil and Gas was formed in 1967 by Moffett and two other partners. Their early success in oil and gas led them to diversify by venturing into copper and gold mining. The company made a series of acquisitions and was renamed Freeport McMoran Incorporated. By 1973, Moffett's mentor, Darrell Royal, had forged his own success by winning three national championships in college football. Meanwhile, Jim Bob's company was opening the world's largest gold mine in Indonesia.

By the late 1980s, Coach Royal had been absent from the sidelines for a decade. He had served as Assistant to then-President of UT, William H. Cunningham. Life was good for Darrell and Edith. They had never led an extravagant life. During his coaching career, Royal never made much money. Both he and Edith put a premium on their love of people. While they each relished being the center of attention, holding that position allowed Darrell to succeed at raising considerable money for UT. Later, he played golf in charity fundraisers with celebrities like Bob Hope, Willie Nelson, Larry Gatlin, and others.

Around the same time, the nation's savings and loans hit a crisis point. Over 1,000 savings and loans failed because of unregulated, risky real estate ventures. The Federal Savings and Loan Insurance Corporation (FSLIC) and the Resolution Trust Company (RTC) protected depositors while disposing of tens of thousands of real estate holdings that had been used as loan collateral. Jim Bob Moffett and his wife were living in New Orleans even though his heart was in Austin. Now, his stunning business successes positioned him to participate in an ambitious real estate play in the city that he loved. Freeport McMoran began to buy up tracts of land located along the banks of Barton Creek in west Austin. FSLIC and RTC were cutting deals to dispose of several thousand acres in the Barton Creek watershed. As is true in all financial crises, the rich find a way to take advantage of others' adversity. In this case, Jim Bob managed to gain control of thousands of acres of raw, hilly real estate that he envisioned as his future retreat for the rich and powerful.

One Saturday morning, Jim Bob made arrangements to come by the Onion Creek home of the Royals and pick them up. He'd told his old coach that he wanted to show them something. When Darrell and Edith climbed into Jim Bob's SUV, they headed out west on Bee Caves Road for a few miles until Jim Bob turned back south toward Barton Creek. They bumped along some rough roads until they arrived high up on a hillside overlooking the creek below. The trio got out of the SUV and Jim Bob retrieved a step ladder from the back. He walked a few yards and set up the step ladder. "Now Edith," he said, "climb up on this ladder." As always, Edith was a good sport. She climbed up as high as she could on the ladder. "Edith, can you see Barton Creek down there?" Yes, Edith said she could. Jim Bob added, "Along the creek is where the first golf course will be. Along the hillsides on both sides, above the golf course, will be home sites with views of the creek and golf course. Now Edith, tell me something. Where do you want your new house to be?" Darrell and Edith grinned with delight. Jim Bob whispered, "Just keep it a secret, okay?"

Sammy Mack Royal was nearing forty years of age. His life had been full of fits and starts. Many times, he surrendered to temptation. A failed marriage. A son, Sammy, was alienated from everyone in the Royal family and was living somewhere in Europe. Darrell and Edith really didn't know their grandson. Mack was drifting through life like so many other bohemians who congregated in Austin. However, he was a bright guy full of ideas and a passionate John Kennedy assassination conspiracy theorist. Mack's theories implicated high officials, including Texans he had met along the way. It was clear that Mack, whatever the subject, instinctively resented authority. Historic preservation and environmental concerns mobilized him to protest and occasionally to support legal action. After all, protest had been counter-culture methodology since the anti-war movement of the 1960s. When the Barton Creek development group began the process of platting, permitting, and environmental assessment through the City of Austin, the counterculture went into action. Protestors showed up in droves for public meetings in an effort to derail the project. They passionately believed that destroying the wilderness along Barton Creek would ultimately destroy the watershed downstream toward the City of Austin, and most importantly, Barton Springs. The springs were a natural treasure fed by water flowing through Barton Creek before turning underground through limestone channels and resulting in natural springs. Water quality, wildlife habitats and marine life were in danger, the protestors declared, all because of greedy, powerful developers. The developers countered with their own studies which found, predictably, no environmental risk related into what had grown to a 9,000 acre development.

At a public hearing, the room was packed to capacity with protestors. Among those signing in to speak against the project was Mack Royal. Mack says today, "I saw Jim Bob Moffett across the room with some other suits, but I wasn't acquainted with him." When Mack's turn came to speak, he identified himself as the son of former UT football coach, Darrell Royal. Then he proceeded to contest the notion that west Austin needed to be turned over to greedy developers with total disregard for the public good or nature's preservation. Jim Bob Moffett eventually got an opportunity to answer such declarations. Some days later, Mack went over to his parents' house to tell them what he'd done. After he told Darrell about the hearing, Darrell shrieked, "You did WHAT?" Jim Bob's old coach put his head in his hands in despair.

During this period of time, when the proposed Barton Creek development was attracting a torrent of controversy, UT President Cunningham had agreed to name a new building on the Forty Acres after Jim Bob Moffett and his then-wife Louise in return for a one-million dollar gift. Darrell Royal may have been the intermediary. Cunningham was simultaneously serving as a paid director of Freeport McMoran. In 1997, the Louise and Jim Bob Moffett Molecular Biology Building was complete.

The *Austin Chronicle* is a left-leaning weekly alternative newspaper which fearlessly tackles sensitive political and social issues in the community. The September 23, 2005, issue of the *Chronicle*, included a scathing article about Jim Bob Moffett, entitled "Written in Stone." In addition to the obvious conflict of interest between the University of Texas, President Cunningham, and Freeport McMoran's development interests, the article described in provocative detail the devastating environmental consequences associated with Freeport's Grasberg Indonesian mining operation and ancillary human rights violations inflicted upon the local Indonesian people. In regard to Moffett, the article states, "We're accustomed to seeing from Moffett cronyism, environmental degradation, and lousy corporate governance. In other words, business as usual." Freeport operated on such a large scale that it could simply outlast its vocal opponents. Henry Kissinger had been Freeport's consultant on international affairs. Former U.S. Ambassador to Indonesia, Stapleton Roy, had been managing director of Kissinger & Associates. Consulting contracts between Freeport and political heavyweights sprung up everywhere. A reading of Sanford Levinson's *Written in Stone: Public Monuments in Changing Societies* is essential to understanding Moffett.

Controversy temporarily subsided when the phone rang at the Royal home in the early hours of March, 1982. A doctor at Brackenridge Hospital was calling to tell the Royals that their youngest child, David Wade, was in a motorcycle crash. David's motorcycle had veered off the Mo-Pac Expressway and hit a road sign while traveling at high speed. David, always the daredevil, had suffered internal injuries which proved fatal. David's death at the age of 29 was another crushing blow. The Royals had lost their only daughter and now, their younger son, to violent accidents. In 1983, the remaining child, Mack, was effectively living in exile.

Then came the news that a young Hispanic woman, "Beany" Trombetta, was carrying David's child. For a time, Darrell turned his back on the traumas of the past. Edith, always the nurturer, couldn't do that. When the infant Elena was born, Edith found it comforting to hold her granddaughter and think of David. Eventually little Elena was fully integrated into the Royal clan. All the pain of loss somehow brought the Royal family and the Kazen family close once again. The grandkids made life tolerable.

In 1980, Frank Erwin passed away suddenly on October 1 while visiting Galveston. Darrell no longer felt the need to watch his back. Erwin's potent influence over UT Regents and Presidents was over. After his death, Frank Erwin's body lay in state at the LBJ Library. Erwin is the only person other than President Johnson to be accorded the honor. There was an explanation. Frank Erwin had quietly arranged for Tina Houston, the wife of his stepson, to serve as Deputy Director of the Library.

Darrell's work as a fundraiser for UT made sense. The fact that he never held a regular job after the age of 52 was peculiar but explainable. He didn't need to work. His job description involved pressing the flesh with potential donors at cocktail parties, attending charity events around the State, presenting and receiving awards on behalf of UT, and most importantly, preaching the gospel of Texas exceptionality. According to recent statistics, the University of Texas System ranks only behind Harvard and Yale among colleges ranked by size of their endowments. Darrell may well have viewed his task as just another form of recruiting. Instead of football players, he was recruiting cash.

The Royals traveled extensively in the State of Texas in this enterprise, rubbing elbows with celebrities and posing for photo ops. Playing golf in support of charitable causes was a relaxing way to live out the fourth quarter of Darrell's life. Johnny Thompson, scion of the 7-11 convenience store chain through the Southland Corporation, had been a friend of the Royals since the 1960's. Every summer the Royals were handed the keys to the palatial Thompson retreat in Cuernavaca, Mexico. Cuernavaca, located south of Mexico City, was the Mexican equivalent of Havana for the country's elite. As such, it attracted the rich and powerful from the United States. It is said Clint Murchison had an estate nearby. It is also said that Sam "Momo" Giancana, the notorious mob kingpin, had an estate in Cuernavaca. The Thompson estate was large enough for the Royals to invite other friends and family to spend a month with them. Everyone was welcome. Good times and happy memories were made there, as family photos reflect. Darrell played golf. The ladies lounged by the pool with servants catering to their needs. The younger ones rode burros and explored the city. Young David Royal bought himself a parrot named Pat which he took home to Austin. Pat became conversationally bilingual. Today, Mack Royal calls his modest Austin home "Cuernavaca."

Cuernavaca wasn't the Royals' only tropical destination. After Lyndon Johnson left the presidency in 1968, his appetite for political life remained ingrained. An endless stream of visitors made their way to the LBJ Ranch located west of Austin near Johnson City. Years earlier, Coach Royal accommodated the former President by bringing a couple of his star players out to the ranch for lunch with Johnson. In 1971 and again in 1972, the Royals joined the Johnsons for a vacation in Acapulco, Mexico. It seems the former President of Mexico had a resort home there and made it available to Johnson. Darrell admitted to feeling awkward in those poolside discussions about foreign policy and the national economy. He saw himself as a football coach and nothing more. Occasionally, the conversations were further complicated by Frank Erwin's presence.

Jimmy Dean grew up in Plainview, Texas. While he never attended the University of Texas, he was a Longhorn fan through and through. Darrell Royal and Jimmy Dean became good friends through their mutual interest in Texas football and country music. Jimmy Dean rose to the top of the entertainment industry in 1961 with the release of his song, "Big Bad John." Dean's popularity led to the production of his national variety show, *The Jimmy Dean Show*. Dean brought country music into the homes of Americans in a new and different way. The show ran from 1963 through 1966. Many entertainers owe their careers to Jimmy Dean. The first appearance of Jim Henson's Muppets happened on Dean's show. George Jones, Buck Owens, Charlie Rich, and Roger Miller all appeared alongside the affable Dean. Darrell Royal's days running with Jimmy Dean on his tour bus were both comfortable and exciting. In 1969, Jimmy and his brother Don started the Jimmy Dean Sausage Company. Dean's downhome charm made the sausage an instant hit. Eventually, Darrell obtained considerable shares of stock in the sausage company. When Dean sold his sausage empire to the Sara Lee Corporation in 1984, it was a windfall for stockholders. Jimmy Dean was now a wealthy man. He donated a million dollars to tiny Wayland Baptist University in his home town of Plainview, Texas simply because it felt good to do so.

Frank Denius is described as "the ultimate booster" in the May 31, 2012 issue of the official publication of the Texas Exes, a UT alumni group. Denius still plays that role today. Darrell Royal, until the time of his death, dutifully maintained a close relationship with Denius. There is, however, much to understand about Frank Denius. Former Texas Governor Rick Perry described Denius as "a war hero, . . . a philanthropist, a lawyer, a businessman, and I might add, the biggest UT fan that I know." While Perry has a penchant for exaggeration, he was accurate with regard to Denius.

In his book *The Big Rich: The Rise and Fall of the Greatest Texas Oil Fortunes*, Bryan Burrough offers further insight. Once again, Burrough's work describes Texas wealth through Wofford Cain. Cain was a native of Athens, Texas and was Sid Richardson's and Clint Murchison's protégé. World War II generated enormous demand for crude oil to power the Allied efforts in Europe, North Africa, and the South Pacific. Richardson and Murchison made their fortunes in the discovery and production of oil. Cain found his fortune, first, in pipelining. The vast oil reserves in West Texas had to be transported overland to the refineries on the Texas gulf coast and in Louisiana. Deepwater ports transported diesel fuel and gasoline to power the war effort. The Southern Pipeline Company was an important cog in the overall picture. In fact, over the next half century, Southern Pipeline morphed into one of the world's largest utility companies. Today, the Southern Company is a vertically integrated electric utility firm with multiple subsidiaries from the original web of piplelines, to coal-fired generating plants, to nuclear power and electric distribution systems. What Wofford Cain started brought fabulous wealth to his descendants. Wofford Cain died in 1977, married but childless. His nephew was Frank Denius, the war hero.

After his military service in World War II ended, Denius obtained his business and law degrees from UT. Doing so helped him establish himself in Austin and later in Texas. Denius joined an Austin law firm but his primary responsibility after 1952 was as director of the Cain Foundation. The Cain Foundation was born years earlier out of Wofford Cain's fortune. Recent filings reflect annual earnings between ten and fifty million dollars a year. Board director Frank Denius decides which charitable entities will receive gifts from the foundation. Over the last forty years, Denius has maintained his own law office while he oversees foundation activities and allows nothing to get in the way of his regular attendance at Longhorn football practices and games. He has been honored many times by UT in various ways including the establishment of Frank Denius Memorial Plaza on the football stadium grounds. Frank Denius has also been honored for his heroism as a soldier. His luck, however, was the accident of his birth into Wofford Cain's extended family. Frank Denius paid homage to his uncle in the most personal way possible. His son's name? Wofford Denius.

In the 1980s, Joe Jamail used to ride over to Austin from his home in Houston with Hugh Liedtke and Liedtke's wife to attend UT football games. Jamail was already a hard-charging Houston trial lawyer with a larger-than-life personality, a penchant for salty language, and a sharp wit. Jamail was fun to be around. Brothers Bill and Hugh Liedtke weren't Texans at all. They were born and raised in Tulsa, Oklahoma. Tulsa was known as the oil capital of the world during the first half of the twentieth century. When U.S. Senator Prescott Bush of Connecticut wanted to place his son George H. W. Bush in a profitable career in the oil business, he called Hugh Liedtke. Liedtke recommended that young George and his wife Barbara relocate to Midland, Texas, where the Liedtke brothers had just opened a law office. George began his education about the rough and tumble world of the west Texas oil business by selling oil field equipment. Eventually the Liedtke brothers and George Bush organized the Zapata Corporation, a fledgling oil and gas firm. They later acquired South Penn Oil Company which they merged with Zapata. They then changed the company name to Pennzoil.

By the 1980s the Liedtke brothers had relocated Pennzoil to the new oil capital of the world, Houston, Texas. From there, George Bush began a political career that would eventually lead all the way to the White House. Today, George and Barbara reside in Houston. By chance, Hugh Liedtke complained to Joe Jamail that he was getting screwed by Texaco regarding an oil contract Pennzoil had negotiated with Getty Oil. Liedtke was unhappy that a major oil company like Texaco could steamroll Pennzoil and ignore the contract

terms which Getty had verbally accepted prior to being acquired by
Texaco. Jamail was no expert in the oil business, but he understood
contract law. Even so, he wasn't optimistic that Liedtke had a winna-
ble case. Jamail eventually changed his mind. When the verdict came
in, Pennzoil was awarded 12.1 billion dollars. Jamail's attorney fees
amounted to a mere 345 million. Joe Jamail had become a legendary
trial lawyer, with this single verdict. When he needed heart surgery,
another UT grad and an icon in his field, Doctor Denton Cooley,
not only performed Jamail's surgery but drove Joe home himself.
According to ESPN's online magazine, when Jamail arrived home
from the hospital along with Doctor Cooley, his friend Darrell Royal
was there waiting for him. In the related interview, Jamail told the
ESPN reporter that Royal was a dear friend and that he had even
taken him on a recruiting trip. When the ill-mannered eighteen-year
old recruit demanded that Jamail promise he could get him admitted
to UT Law School, Jamail's days as a UT recruiter were over. These
days, when Edith feels up to attending a UT home football game, she
sits next to Jamail in his suite and watches the action below played
out on Joe Jamail Field.

Billy Joe "Red" McCombs earned his initial fortune selling cars.
The McCombs Auto Group now has dozens of dealerships. However,
Red's interests far exceed automobiles. He became a principal in
Clear Channel Communications, a national chain of radio stations.
Later, he owned at different times the San Antonio Spurs, the Denver
Nuggets, and the Minnesota Vikings. He is currently serving as
Chairman of the Constellis Group, a web of shadowy entities pro-
viding "security services" to government agencies, private corporations, and non-governmental organizations around the world. The
dangerous world of cyber terrorism, kidnappings, bombings, and
intellectual property theft makes people anxious. For those that can
afford it, the Constellis affiliate Triple Canopy and the highly controversial Blackwater organization are available. The name Blackwater
has been dropped to conceal the company's negative image. The
company is now known as Academi. Blackwater operatives at one
time were held accountable for the deaths of seventeen Iraqi civilians

plus twenty injured during a breakdown of discipline while on duty in Baghdad. All of these entities are overseen by Red McCombs. Academi is a mercenary force consisting of former Rangers, Delta Force, and Navy Seals who conduct operations outside the purview of an inquiring U.S. Congress. When governments move too slowly or not at all, Academi moves in. Contracts for such services bring in hundreds of millions of dollars. The work is dangerous and possibly illegal. But war is messy. And highly profitable.

McCombs' current estimated net worth is 1.85 billion dollars according to *Forbes Magazine*. The millions he has donated to UT are reflected in the UT Business School named for him. He's an opinionated, quotable fellow. When UT hired Charlie Strong as head football coach, in 2014, McCombs offered his thoughts to a radio interviewer, perhaps on one of his own stations. In that interview, which McCombs gave only days after Strong was hired, McCombs questioned Strong's capabilities. He told the interviewer he didn't think Strong was ready to take on a head job of the size and complexity of UT. Those comments made national news. They were interpreted nationwide as racist. UT had long fought against their image as an elitist educational institution unwelcoming to blacks. Within a few days, McCombs was backtracking publicly but the damage had already been done.

The empire that became Texas Longhorn football began with Darrell Royal but it certainly won't end there. New overlords will take the place of Erwin, Moffett, Jamail, Denius, McCombs and others. Coach Royal had the ability to adapt to whatever circumstances confronted him. He became a coaching legend and in doing so, also became a Texas icon. He was comfortable with all of it. When he was interviewed by author John Wheat for the 2005 oral history, *Coach Royal: Conversations with a Texas Football Legend*, Wheat devoted an entire chapter to Royal's relationship with Jim Bob Moffett. In the chapter, Royal offers a spirited defense of his long relationship with the controversial business tycoon and specifically of Moffett's efforts to develop Barton Creek Properties. Royal had no background in environmental matters, hydrology, or land use. Despite that, he had a favorable opinion of Jim Bob's vision for a west Austin retreat for the elite. Darrell told Wheat, "I serve as the Chairman of the Board out there because of Jim Bob. He got me involved. He's the CEO of Freeport McMoran and they've been very generous with their money." Indeed they had. Coach Royal didn't share with Wheat how that he and Edith had come by their hillside residence in Barton Creek.

Forbes Magazine touts the athletic department at the University of Texas as the most valuable in all of college sports. To achieve that status, the department had to be run like a business—a very large, lucrative business. Something comparable to Freeport McMoran. Or Academi.

Until his health began to fail in 2010, Darrell and Edith Royal lived a comfortable life and managed to cope with the sorrows of their family losses. When Darrell's memory was lost to Alzheimer's, they moved into a lavish retirement complex near the Omni Barton Creek Resort. When Darrell felt up to it, they would drive over to the club for lunch. Darrell could gaze on the many framed pictures of himself in happier times. He could touch his own statue near the golf clubhouse. No other college coach has been so regally and completely honored. Darrell K Royal—Texas Memorial Stadium stands as a testament to that.

Edith is alone now, except for the regular visits from her grandkids and great grandkids. She dotes on them, as any grandmother would. So many of her friends are gone now. She is a spry and sharp eighty-nine years old. She enjoys talking about the old days in Hollis, their many stops along the coaching trail, Austin, and the Longhorns. "I remember," she says with a smile, "when Darrell joined a group of men flying by private jet to Raleigh-Durham, North Carolina, to meet Mack Brown." Mack was then the head coach of the North Carolina Tar Heels. Brown was in the crosshairs of these Texas overlords. They needed someone to take over a Texas football program that had been anemic for twenty years. There was a true sense of urgency in this cross country trip. When Darrell got home late that night, Edith met him at the door. "How'd you all do?" Darrell grinned and said, "We got him. But really, Edie, there was never any doubt. We had enough money on that plane to BUY North Carolina!"

Darrell passed away November 7, 2012. His massive funeral was held, ironically, in the Frank Erwin Center. One year later, Mack Brown had fallen out of favor at UT. Within three months, the Texas overlords fired Bill Powers, President of UT; DeLoss Dodds, Athletic Director at UT; and Coach Mack Brown. By that time, Darrell was resting in the Texas State Cemetery in east Austin, not far from the likes of Governor John Connally, Frank Erwin, Governor Ann Richards, and Governor Alan Shivers. The beautiful hillside cemetery reserved for notable Texans—and one young man from Hollis, Oklahoma, who had become a Texas Caesar.

Mack Royal

EPILOGUE

Our home phone in Oklahoma City was ringing three or four times a day. I'd answer and Darrell would say, "Donnie, how ya doin?" I'd tell him, "Hello, Darrell. I'm just sittin' here with Melba decidin' what we want for lunch." One time Darrell said, "You remember that time you took your grandpa's pickup out late one night without permission and we went joy ridin' up and down Main Street? Guys would yell at us to let 'em ride in the bed of the pickup. That one fella came up and we told him he could ride. Then when he started to get in, you hit the gas and we sped off. That guy picked up a rock and threw it at us and broke out the back glass of the pickup. Boy, we were in trouble then! But I got my brother Ray out of bed to come down to his mechanic shop and put in a new rear glass. It was good as new before the sun came up. Your grandpa never knew a thing about it! Remember that?"

The phone calls and stories from our days as kids in Hollis kept coming. After a week or so, I called Edith and told her about Darrell's phone calls. I was concerned she might not like that, being long distance and all. She said, "Donnie, you talk to him as much as he wants to. It's okay."

I knew he was getting close to the end. I wanted to see him one last time. One of my boys had a motorhome, so we planned a road trip to Austin. Edith said she and Darrell would meet us at the Barton Creek Club for lunch. When we got there, I could see why she chose the place. There were pictures and trophies and memorabilia of the Darrell K Royal those Texans knew everywhere. Edith gave us a tour. There was even a statue of Darrell outside by the golf shop. People down there thought Darrell was really somethin'.

After lunch, we sat down to visit in a beautiful spot in the club. Edith sat on a couch close to Darrell. He didn't talk much at all. It was clear he couldn't follow the conversation very well. Edith kept it going, talking about old times back home. We were having a good time. Then suddenly, Darrell piped up and said, "Edie, I want to go home to Hollis." She squeezed his hand and said, "Now honey, these boys have come down here to see you. We've got Hollis right here!" Darrell looked at us through those soft, puzzled eyes. After a moment, he said, "Is that all that's left of Hollis?"

Don Fox
January, 2015

Pioneer Women of the Oklahoma Territory. The great aunts of Edith Thomason Royal

Darrell Royal and friend outside Cecil Sumpter's Barber Shop, Hollis, Oklahoma, circa 1940.

Darrell Royal and fellow airmen of the Army Air Corps, Tampa Air Field, where Darrell trained as a B-24 tail gunner, circa 1944.

Darrell Royal kisses his son, Mack, goodbye before boarding a Braniff Airways plane for the Oklahoma Sooners game against the U.S. Military Academy in West Point, New York, played September 28, 1946.

Oklahoma Sooner halfback Darrell Royal sweeps around right end for a touchdown, 1948.

Marion and Mack Royal are tended to by their nanny/housekeeper, Starkville, Mississippi, circa 1954.

Coach Dana X. Bible's admonition to Darrell to avoid the State Capitol proved impossible to do. The eyes of Texas came to Coach Royal, circa 1960.

The revolution in Austin, Texas came abruptly, on multiple levels. Coach Royal's Longhorns won UT's first national football championship in the fall 1963, days after President Kennedy was assassinated in Dallas; Texan Lyndon Johnson was sworn in as President; and anti-war student protests advanced on the UT campus.

A prominent statue on the UT campus of Jefferson Davis, President of the Confederacy, summons up a history of Texas' 1846 secession in the name of slavery; 123 years later, UT's 1969 football national champion players were all white.

Post-World War II college football coaches made very little money. The unique Texas culture, however, has always taken care of its own. Darrell Royal, Earl Campbell and Jim Bob Moffett in happier days, circa 1990.

Left to right, Sammy Mack, David Wade and Marian K Royal circa 1962. Neither David nor Marian would live to see thirty. Mack survives today.

Frank C. Erwin, as Chairman of the UT Board of Regents, ruled UT-Austin as his personal fiefdom. Anyone who got in his way would be crushed eventually.

Tulsa native Hugh Liedtke, President of Pennzoil, is joined by his attorney, Joe Jamail and friend Darrell Royal in celebrating a multi-billion dollar judgment against Texaco over a contract dispute. Today, the Texas Longhorns play on Joe Jamail Field.

Darrell Royal's resting place in the Texas State Cemetery in Austin.

155

.

44918012R00105

Made in the USA
San Bernardino, CA
24 July 2019